# Excel University
# Volume 2 -
## Featuring Excel 2016 for Windows

A walk-through of the Excel® features, functions and techniques that improve the productivity of accountants.

During his live CPE training sessions, Jeff Lenning CPA CITP has shown thousands of CPAs and Accounting Professionals across the country how to use Excel more effectively and how to leverage Excel to improve efficiency and reduce the time it takes to complete job tasks. This series of books is a comprehensive collection of the features, functions, and techniques that are of direct benefit to accountants working in industry, public practice, consulting, or the nonprofit sector. Each book in the Excel University series includes narrative, screenshots, Excel practice files, and video content. This series uses a hands-on approach to learning, and provides practice files and exercises that demonstrate the practical application of the items presented in each chapter.

## JEFF LENNING, CPA CITP
## EXCEL UNIVERSITY, INC.

**Excel University – Volume 2**
By: Jeff Lenning CPA CITP
Version: 3.0

All rights reserved.
Copyright © 2017 by Jeff Lenning

ISBN-10: 1543187218
EAN-13: 9781543187212

# About the Author

In his live CPE training sessions, Jeff Lenning, CPA CITP, has shown thousands of CPAs and accounting professionals across the country how to use Excel to streamline their work and become more efficient. His Excel articles have been featured in several publications, including the *Journal of Accountancy* and *California CPA Magazine*. He is the founder of Excel University, Inc., a firm that specializes in Excel training. Jeff graduated from the University of Southern California.

# EXCEL UNIVERSITY RESOURCES

## EXCEL UNIVERSITY VIDEO LIBRARY

✓ excel-university.com/videos

## EXCEL UNIVERSITY DOWNLOAD LIBRARY

✓ excel-university.com/downloads

## EXCEL UNIVERSITY BLOG

✓ excel-university.com

## INTERACTIVE ONLINE TRAINING VERSION OF THIS VOLUME

✓ excel-university.com/training

# Contents at a Glance

# Table of Contents

# OPENING INFORMATION

*Excel is my favorite computer application of all time.
My goal is to help you maximize its power.*

# Chapter 1: Overview

## WELCOME BACK!

I'm so glad you've decided to continue on to the next volume in the Excel University series. We covered the foundations in the first volume, and it's now time to build on that knowledge. I refer to Volume 1 as the "Foundations" book, and I refer to this volume as the "Hands-Free Reporting" book.

## HANDS-FREE REPORTING

In this volume we explore the Excel features and functions needed to build reports that update their values automatically, and I use the terms *hands-off*, *hands-free*, and *paste-and-go* throughout the series to describe this concept. Hands-off reporting was briefly introduced in Volume 1 and describes a formula-based report whose values update when new data is pasted into the workbook.

 **XREF**

> Hands-off reporting is discussed in Volume 1, Chapters 15 and 16.

We'll cover the individual functions needed, and then apply many of them at once to build hands-free reports. The final chapter models my preferred structure for reporting workbooks and illustrates how to separate the data from the report, check for errors, and provide interactive and dynamic reports to users without the use of macros.

Hands-free reporting has transformed my work life and enabled me to complete my reporting tasks much faster. It is my goal that the ideas presented here will be as valuable to you.

## MASLOW'S HAMMER

How do you get to work? Assuming you work outside your home, how do you physically travel from your home to your office? Do you walk? Ride a bike? Drive a car? Technically, all three of these travel methods would get you from your home to your office and achieve the goal. However, the speed with which you accomplish your goal depends entirely on the approach selected.

Likewise, you'll find that Excel usually offers several approaches to accomplish any given task, but some get you there faster than others. I'll present various methods to achieve the same task, because often the most efficient method depends on the context of the data, structure, and workbook.

Have you ever heard of the law of the instrument, also known as Maslow's hammer? It is the idea of overreliance on a familiar tool. There are many variants, but a common phrasing of the concept is

*If all you have is a hammer, everything looks like a nail.*

To me, this implies that a limited selection of tools reduces your options and effectiveness. One of my goals is to expand your options greatly by presenting a wide range of functions. I hope that after you work through the exercises, you'll have a deep and comprehensive understanding of the functions presented and will know when and how to integrate them into your workbooks. I want you to have more tools so you can pick the right one for the job.

In this volume, we address a task common to many accounting professionals: reporting. We'll explore various Excel functions that make report preparation more efficient. Because formula-based reports are prepared primarily with formulas and functions rather than Excel features, they have very little, if any, structural limits. Therefore you can prepare formula-based reports with virtually any layout, design, or format.

In hands-free reports, the workbook is organized so that the data sheet is separate from the report sheet. This is important, so allow me to restate the point:

*Hands-free reporting workbooks store data on one worksheet and the report on another worksheet.*

Splitting the data from the report is a critical design consideration, especially for recurring-use workbooks, because to update the report next period, all we need to do is paste the new data into the data sheet, and the formulas instantly recalculate the report values. After we explore formula-based reports in this volume, we'll cover PivotTable reports in the next volume. I love the PivotTable feature—it may even be my favorite. However, because PivotTables impose limitations on a report's structure, I decided to discuss formula-based reports first, as they are flexible and have almost no structure limitations. PivotTables do have the distinct advantage of automatically expanding themselves to include any new items in the list, whereas, formula-based reports don't, and you need to add new rows manually for any new items.

Even if you are not involved in reporting, the functions covered in this volume have many other uses that you will likely find valuable.

## BOOK CONVENTIONS

Let's quickly review the conventions used throughout the Excel University series.

### REFERENCES

You'll encounter the following references throughout the text:

**DEPENDS ON** — The item being presented depends on an item previously presented.

**XREF** — A cross reference to a related or complementary item.

**NOTE** — A general note about the item being presented.

**KB** — The keyboard shortcut or shortcuts used to perform the task.

**PRACTICE** — A reference to the exercise workbook and worksheet.

**VIDEO** — A reference to the realated video contenet.

### STYLE CONVENTIONS

Formulas are presented in monospaced font, as follows:

```
=SUM(A1:A10)
```

Any additional information about the formula or function is explained immediately after the formula.

## CHAPTER STRUCTURE

In general, the following chapters contain these sections:

- Set Up—Provides an overview and highlights the benefits and uses.

- How To—Details how to implement the feature or function.

- Examples—Suggest hands-on exercises that illustrate an application of the feature or function.

## CORRECTIONS AND SUGGESTIONS

If you find any errors in the book or the exercise workbooks, please let me know so that I can correct them in the next revision. Send a note to info@excel-university.com.

Also, if you have any suggestions for content, additional application of presented features or functions, or anything else that you think should be incorporated into this text, please let me know.

## SUCCESS STORIES

I love to hear success stories, which make me all warm and fuzzy inside and provide me with inspiration and motivation. Please take a moment to share your process improvements, especially those tasks that now take less time. Drop a note to info@excel-university.com.

# EXCEL CONVENTIONS

Throughout this text, I've referred to navigation through the Ribbon user interface as follows:

Ribbon Tab Name > Button Name

## EXCEL VERSIONS

The screenshots in this text were captured with Microsoft Excel 2016 for Windows. For the most part, I note in the text how to navigate to a feature using the Ribbon and Button names. Not all features and functions discussed in this text are available in older versions of Excel. Additionally, features presented in this text may not be available in other versions of Excel, such as Excel Online, Excel for Mac, or mobile versions.

# HOW TO MAKE THE MOST

Here are my thoughts about how to make the most of our time together and maximize the benefits of working through the Excel University series.

## WORKBOOK DOWNLOAD

In my opinion, the best way to learn Excel is by hands-on experience, and I have provided sample Excel workbooks that you can use to gain that experience. Each workbook has a worksheet named Start Here, which lists each exercise and its purpose. The exercise sheets are incomplete. You complete the exercise by writing a formula or function or by using a feature. These workbooks aren't provided as a reference—rather, they are designed for you to work through and complete.

The exercises attempt to demonstrate the application of each feature and function in a relevant and practical way.

Please feel free to download the workbooks from the following:

### www.excel-university.com/downloads

The download is a single Zip file containing all of the Excel files. Extract the Zip file to gain access to the practice files.

## *ANSWERS VERSION*

You'll notice that there are essentially two versions of each workbook:

- The exercise version is referenced by name in this text. It provides space to write the formulas and otherwise complete various exercises included in the workbook.

- The answers version is denoted with _answers appended to the workbook name. It contains the completed exercises and formulas.

## *EXTRA CREDIT*

Some exercise workbooks have Extra Credit worksheets. As a rule, the sheets named Exercise are demonstrated in this text. The Extra Credit worksheets carry the feature beyond what is presented in this text, providing additional examples and illustrations. The answers for the Extra Credit exercises are included in the answers version of each workbook.

## MY FAVORITES

As you progress through this series, it may be helpful to list the items that are the most relevant to you and that you want to implement into your workbooks. Feel free to make notes of those items in the My Favorites table that follows.

# MY FAVORITES

*Feel free to make a note of features or functions that you want to remember to practice and implement into your workbooks as you work through the content.*

| PAGE | TOPIC |
|------|-------|
|      |       |
|      |       |
|      |       |
|      |       |
|      |       |
|      |       |
|      |       |
|      |       |
|      |       |
|      |       |
|      |       |
|      |       |
|      |       |
|      |       |
|      |       |
|      |       |
|      |       |
|      |       |
|      |       |
|      |       |
|      |       |
|      |       |
|      |       |
|      |       |
|      |       |
|      |       |
|      |       |
|      |       |
|      |       |
|      |       |

| PAGE | TOPIC |
|------|-------|
|      |       |
|      |       |
|      |       |
|      |       |
|      |       |
|      |       |
|      |       |
|      |       |
|      |       |
|      |       |
|      |       |
|      |       |
|      |       |
|      |       |
|      |       |
|      |       |
|      |       |
|      |       |
|      |       |
|      |       |
|      |       |
|      |       |
|      |       |
|      |       |
|      |       |
|      |       |
|      |       |
|      |       |
|      |       |
|      |       |
|      |       |
|      |       |
|      |       |
|      |       |
|      |       |
|      |       |
|      |       |
|      |       |
|      |       |

# Chapter 2: Selected Shortcuts

## SET UP

In Excel University—Volume 1, we explored five selected shortcuts that I hope you've been using. If so, your muscles have memorized them, you don't need to think about them, and they are now second nature. As a quick reminder, here are the Volume 1 shortcuts:

1. Arrow keys for navigation.

2. F2 for edit mode.

3. F4 for reference styles: absolute, relative, and mixed.

4. Double-click to fill down.

5. Ctrl+PageUp/PageDown to switch sheets.

 **XREF**

Selected shortcuts are discussed in Volume 1, Chapter 6.

Since we'll be writing a ton of formulas in this volume, I'm providing some relevant shortcuts that I hope will also become second nature.

1. F9 and related formula shortcuts.

2. Fill down and right.

3. Ctrl+Home to jump to A1.

4.Row shortcuts.

5.Column shortcuts.

# HOW TO

Let's kick off our shortcuts discussion with the F9 key and also revisit a few selected shortcuts discussed in the first volume.

## F9 AND RELATED FORMULA SHORTCUTS

The F9 key has several uses in Excel. Right now, I'd like to focus on how it can help when working on formulas:

- F9 will immediately evaluate selected formula text and replace it with the result.

This is very helpful when troubleshooting formulas or understanding new formulas you encounter. Let's say your formula isn't working as expected, or the formula is long and complex and you want to better understand a portion of it. Simply highlight the desired formula text and press F9. Excel will replace the selected string with the computed result. Please note that after converting the selected text, you need to press the Escape (Esc) key to prevent the conversion from becoming permanent. If you press Enter instead of Escape, the conversion will be permanent. Of course, you can undo this change if needed.

As a simple example, consider this formula:

```
=ROUND(SUM(A1:A5),2)
```

If we enter Edit mode, either by selecting the formula cell and pressing F2 or by double-clicking the cell, we can highlight a portion of the formula such as the SUM function, as shown here:

```
=ROUND(SUM(A1:A5),2)
```

Pressing the F9 key tells Excel to evaluate the selected portion of the formula immediately and replace it with the result. Assuming that the sum of the range A1:A5 is 10, pressing F9 causes Excel to update the formula as follows:

```
=ROUND(10,2)
```

At this point, if you wanted to keep the original SUM function in the formula, then you would want to press the Escape key so the change is not permanent. If you press the Enter key instead of the Escape key, then the change would be stored.

F9 offers a fast technique for troubleshooting formulas or figuring out how they work.

Since we'll be writing so many formulas in this volume, I will review and expand on a couple of shortcuts we covered in the first volume.

## F4

Remember that pressing the F4 key while editing a formula cycles the cell reference at the cursor through the various relative and absolute options.

## F2

When you press F2 while a cell is selected, Excel will enter Edit mode and place the cursor inside the cell formula or value. This is a fast way to edit formulas. Now let's expand this discussion a bit.

Did you know Excel has different operating modes? You can tell which Excel mode you are in by examining the status label in the lower left corner of the Excel window. Typically, Excel is in Ready mode. If you look at your Excel screen now, that is probably what you'll see in the lower left corner. When you are in Ready mode, the arrow keys navigate you from cell to cell. Other modes include Edit, Enter, and Point.

When you edit a formula, Excel flips to Edit mode, and the mode status in the lower left corner of Excel will say Edit. You get into Edit mode by pressing F2, double-clicking a cell that contains a formula or value, or clicking inside the formula bar. In Edit mode, the arrow keys navigate within the formula text. For example, the Left Arrow will move the cursor one character to the left, and so on. Go ahead and try this in Excel now.

Enter mode is different from Edit mode. If you go to a blank cell and enter something, for example, an equal sign to begin writing a formula, you'll notice that you are operating in Excel's Enter mode. The status in the lower left corner of Excel changes to Enter. Enter mode is used when entering text into a cell. Go ahead and confirm this now; I'll wait here.

There is something special about Enter mode. Have you ever noticed that when you write a formula, you can use the arrow keys on your keyboard to select cells and ranges, and the selected range is entered into your formula? When a cell reference is expected, using the arrow keys toggles Excel into another operating mode called Point mode. In Point mode, the arrow keys actually leave the formula and navigate the worksheet. The selected cell or range is entered into the formula. Go ahead and try this now: go to a blank cell and type an equal sign. The status changes to Enter mode. Now use the arrow key to navigate to another cell. The status changes to Point mode.

**NOTE**

Here is a challenge for you as you write the formulas in this volume. Try to select cell and range references used in formulas and function arguments with Point mode and the worksheet navigation keyboard commands (arrow keys, Ctrl, and Shift). The exception is when specifying named references and structured table references, since these will appear in the auto-complete list. Doing so will help you keep your hands on the keyboard to improve your speed.

So how does all of this relate back to the F2 key? Here's how: if you navigate to a formula cell and then press F2, you flip into Edit mode. In Edit mode, your arrow keys navigate you within the formula text, and you are sort of trapped in the formula text. If you press F2 again, you toggle into Enter mode, and as you know, in Enter mode when a cell reference is expected, the arrow keys flip you into Point mode so you can navigate to other cells. In essence, you are freed from the formula text, and any cell or ranges references you select are inserted into your formula. Similarly, while in Enter mode, pressing F2 will toggle you into Edit mode. Thus, if you are trying to work on a formula, and you use your arrow keys and accidentally leave the formula text, you can use the F2 key to toggle you into Edit mode where the arrow keys are restricted to moving within the formula text. In summary, remember that

*F2 toggles arrow key navigation between worksheet cells and formula text.*

This same F2 toggle trick works inside of reference fields in dialog boxes as well. For example, if you are working with named ranges, the New Name dialog box allows you to specify a name and then specify a Refers To reference. This Refers To field defaults to Point mode, so that your arrow keys navigate the worksheet rather than navigate the field's text. Hitting the F2 key toggles you into Edit mode so that your arrow keys navigate within the field's text rather than on the worksheet cells.

Here is a summary for reference:

| Mode | Arrow Keys |
|------|------------|
| Ready | Navigate between cells. |
| Enter | Navigate between cells, except when a cell reference is expected in a formula (toggles into Point mode). |
| Edit | Navigate within the characters of the formula or cell value. |
| Point | Navigate between cells. |

**Table 1**

Use F2 to toggle so that you can keep your hands on your keyboard to improve your speed.

## USING AUTO-COMPLETE

Beginning with version 2007, Excel displays an auto-complete list as you enter a function name or named reference into a cell. It is easy to use this list entirely with your keyboard. Basically, as you enter the first few characters of a recognized function name or reference name, you'll see the auto-complete list appear. You can use the Down Arrow and Up Arrow keys to navigate to the desired list item. Pressing the Tab key will enter the selected item into the cell.

## FORMULA TEXT

Here are a couple of pointers for editing formula text. The Left and Right Arrow keys move the cursor or insertion point backward and forward one character at a time. Holding down the Control (Ctrl) key while pressing the Left or Right Arrow key jumps one word at a time. Holding down the Shift key along with an arrow key extends your text selection one character at a time. Holding down both the Shift and the Control keys along with an arrow key extends your selection one word at a time.

Additionally, pressing the End or Home key jumps the cursor to the end or beginning, respectively, of the cell contents, while holding Shift along with End or Home extends the selection to the end or beginning of the formula.

It is also interesting to note the difference between the Delete and Backspace keys. Backspace deletes the character to the left of the cursor, while Delete removes the character to the right of the cursor.

All right, got them? I hope so, because these shortcuts will be quite useful as you crank through the exercise workbooks.

## FILL DOWN AND RIGHT

It is a fairly common practice to write a formula in a cell, and then if it works as expected, fill it down and possibly to the right. We'll repeat this task over and over again, so let's touch on a couple of different approaches.

The first approach, which was presented in Volume 1, is the double-click shortcut. This allows you to double-click in the lower right corner of a formula cell to fill the formula down based on the adjacent column's occupied cells.

Another approach is to first select the formula cell and then extend the selection with your keyboard using the Shift and arrow keys, or Shift and Control plus arrow keys, as discussed at length in Volume 1.

Once the formula cell is active and you have added the destination range to the selection, you can fill down using one of the following techniques.

- If you prefer Control key shortcuts, use Ctrl+D.

- If you prefer Alt key shortcuts, then use Alt+E, I, D (edit, fill, down).

- If you prefer the Ribbon, then use the fill-down button (Home > Fill > Down).

A similar concept applies to filling right. Select the formula cell or range, extend the selection with keyboard commands, and then fill right using one of the following techniques.

- If you prefer Control key shortcuts, use Ctrl+R.

- If you prefer Alt key shortcuts, then use Alt+E, I, R (edit, fill, right).

- If you prefer the Ribbon, then use the fill right button (Home > Fill > Right).

An additional keyboard approach is the standard copy/paste. Copy the formula cell with Ctrl+C, select the destination range using keyboard commands, and then paste using Ctrl+V. Please note that this approach pastes all attributes of the source cell, including both the formula and the formatting. If you want to paste the formula only, perform a Paste Special, Alt+E, S or Ctrl+Alt+V, instead of Paste, and then select Formulas from the Paste Special dialog.

 **NOTE**

When you copy and paste a cell, or copy a cell and then paste special formulas, be aware that the absolute and relative cell references are observed and updated accordingly. However, if you highlight the formula text while in Edit mode, such that you actually copy the formula text rather than the cell contents, and then select the destination cell and paste, the exact formula text is pasted and cell references are not updated.

## CTRL+HOME TO JUMP TO A1

This is a quick shortcut, but one I use quite often. Pressing and holding Ctrl and then pressing the Home key jumps you to cell A1 and makes it the active cell.

## ROW SHORTCUTS

Users frequently perform three row-related tasks:

- Inserting a new row.

- Selecting a row.

- Deleting a row.

The fastest way to perform these tasks is by keeping your hands on the keyboard and using the following shortcuts.

To quickly insert a new row above the active row, range, or cell, use one of the following keyboard shortcuts.

- Alt+I, R (insert, row).

- Alt+H, I ,R (home, insert, row).

Please note that you do not need to select the entire row to use this command. Even if just a single cell is selected, an entire row will be inserted above the active cell. Also note that the number of rows inserted is determined by the number of rows in the current selection. For example, if you select three rows, or if the selected range includes three rows, then the Insert Row command inserts three new rows.

Another common task is to select an entire row, often to delete it. To select an entire row, simply use the following keyboard shortcut.

- Shift+Space.

To delete an entire row, first select the entire row (or rows), and then use one of the following keyboard shortcuts.

- Alt+E, D (edit, delete).

- Ctrl+-

## COLUMN SHORTCUTS

The column shortcuts are about the same as row shortcuts and allow you to insert a column, select an entire column, and delete a column.

To insert a column to the left of the active column, use one of the following shortcuts.

- Alt+I, C (insert, column).

- Alt+H, I, C (home, insert, column).

To select a column, use the following shortcut.

- Ctrl+Space.

To delete a column, use one of the following shortcuts.

- Alt+E, D (edit, delete).

- Ctrl+-

Interestingly, combining the keys to select a column (Ctrl+Space) and a row (Shift+Space) selects all cells in the worksheet. To select all cells in the worksheet, use the following shortcut:

- Ctrl+Shift+Space

For a comprehensive list of shortcuts covered in the Excel University series to date, please refer to the Shortcut Reference near the end of the book.

## EXAMPLES

Let's practice these with some hands-on exercises.

To work along, please refer to *Selected Shortcuts.xlsx*.

To watch the solutions video, please visit the Excel University Video Library.

## EXERCISE 1—F9

In this exercise, we'll use the F9 key to inspect an existing formula.

 **PRACTICE**

To work along, please refer to the Exercise 1 worksheet.

In the worksheet, we compute total sales and then apply the commission rate to the sales in order to compute the total commission. The commission rate is found in cell *C14*, and the total sales amount is found in cell *C28*.

Here is the formula that computes the commission:

=ROUND(C14*C28,0)

**Where:**

- **C14** is the commission rate.

- **C28** is total sales.

Using only our keyboard, we want to spot check the formula. We know that we can highlight any portion of the formula and then press F9 to evaluate the selection and view the results. So, we enter Edit mode for the formula cell, select *C14\*C28*, and then press the F9 key. We observe that Excel evaluates the selection and converts it to 1836.4105. We hit the Escape key so that we don't make this change permanent and so that the formula continues to use cell references.

This shortcut is sure to come in handy.

## EXERCISE 2—CTRL+HOME

This one is easy.

 **PRACTICE**

To work along, please refer to the Exercise 2 worksheet.

Simply use the Ctrl+Home keyboard shortcut to jump to cell *A1*.

## EXERCISE 3—ROW SHORTCUTS

In this exercise, we'll use our keyboard to work with rows.

 **PRACTICE**

To work along, please refer to the Exercise 3 worksheet.

In this workbook, there are some blank rows that we need to remove, so we need to select cells that lie in the rows we wish to delete. Thus we will navigate to a cell in the first row we wish to delete. In this case we can simply navigate to cell *A13*. Next we extend our selection to include the range *A13:A16* by holding down the Shift key and then using the Down Arrow key. Next we select the rows by hitting Shift+Space. Last we use a keyboard command (Alt+E, D) to delete the rows.

Our next task is to insert a new skinny row between the last data row and the Total Sales formula. We simply navigate to any cell in the Total Sales row and use a keyboard shortcut (Alt+I, R) to insert a new row. To change the row height, we use Alt+O, R, E (format, row, height) to bring up the Row Height dialog box and then type 4 and press Enter. We need to update the Total Sales formula to include the new skinny row, so we navigate over to the Total Sales formula cell and press F2 to enter Edit mode. We use the Left Arrow key to move to the left, then we delete the row reference, type in the new row reference, and hit Enter.

If this feels awkward and slow right now, please hang in there with me. Over time this will become second nature, and you'll be happy with how fast you can update your workbooks.

## EXERCISE 4—COLUMN SHORTCUTS

Let's play with columns now.

 **PRACTICE**

To work along, please refer to the Exercise 4 worksheet.

In this worksheet, we need to add a new column for the fourth quarter. We simply use our keyboard to navigate to any cell in the skinny row column, column *G*. Next we insert a new column using our keyboard; I prefer Alt+I, C.

Next we navigate to the column header row and type in our new label: Q4. We now need to fill our Q3 formulas into our Q4 column. We select the Q3 formula cells *F17:F22* and then extend the selection to the right so that the range *F17:G22* is highlighted. Then we fill right. I prefer Alt+E, I, R.

Done…and…done!

## CHAPTER CONCLUSION

If you commit to learn, practice, and use these shortcuts, I'm sure that they will increase your personal productivity.

# CONDITIONAL SUMMING

*Multiple condition summing will rock your world.*

# Chapter 3: Conditional Summing Basics with SUMIFS

## SET UP

It is time to explore one of my favorite Excel functions: SUMIFS. The SUMIFS function was first introduced in Excel 2007, and Microsoft puts it in the Math & Trig function category. It is officially known as a conditional summing function, but that description is too sterile and lacks passion. I prefer to put this function in the *Awesome* category!

A conditional summing function is rather like a SUM function because it adds numbers. It differs from a standard SUM function because it includes only certain cells or rows within the sum range.

Frequently when I use this function, I'm asking Excel to add up a column of numbers but to include only those rows where a specified condition is true. For example, I might want Excel to add up the Amount column but only include those rows where the Department column is equal to 100. Or add up the Quantity column but include only those rows where the Item column is equal to AB349.

Because the samples above have only one condition, they could have been accomplished prior to Excel 2007 with the SUMIF function. However, the SUMIF function has a major limitation in that it can evaluate only a single condition. In practice, it is common to need to evaluate multiple conditions. So Microsoft delivered SUMIFS, which is rather like the plural of SUMIF because it can evaluate multiple conditions, up to 127 to be precise. Now, I strictly use the SUMIFS function, even when I need to evaluate only a single condition, because of its flexible nature and the fact that I can easily add other conditions later.

Using the SUMIFS function, you can easily set up a formula to add up a range but only include those rows where three conditions are met. For example, add up the Amount column, but only include those rows where the Type column is equal to Invoice, the Account column is equal to Telephone Expense, and the Status column is equal to Paid.

By the time you complete this volume, the SUMIFS function will be a familiar friend, since you'll have used it in literally hundreds of cells. Let's now explore the function's syntax.

## HOW TO

The SUMIFS function requires a minimum of three function arguments. The first argument is the range of numbers to add, such as the Amount column. Think about the remaining arguments as pairs. The first in the pair is the criteria *range*, and the second in the pair is the criteria *value*. For example, the Department column would be paired with the department number that the Department column must equal for the row to be included in the total. Another example is the Item column being paired with the Item number. You may specify up to 127 pairs.

The formula is written as follows:

```
=SUMIFS(sum_range, criteria_range1, criteria1,
[criteria_range2], [criteria2], …)
```

**Where:**

- **sum_range** is the range that contains the cells to sum.

- **criteria_range1** is the range to evaluate for this condition.

- **criteria1** is the value that the range must equal to be included in the total.

- …up to 127 total pairs.

It is key to know that when multiple conditions are used, all conditions must be met for the cell to be included in the sum.

To recap, the first argument is the range that contains the cells to add. Then come the criteria arguments expressed in pairs. I can easily remember the order of these arguments when I think about them like this: add up *this column* (argument 1) of numbers, but only include those rows where *this other column* (argument 2) is equal to *this value* (argument 3), and so on.

 **NOTE**

This function works really well on flat data. If your data is not flat, then you probably have blank cells in a column with labels in between, for example, an account column that has the first account label in row 2, and then blank cell values for the next several transactions. This pattern may continue, with the next labels appearing in say rows 10, 15, 23, and so on, with blank cells in between the labels. A fast way to fill these values down into the blank cells, is to select the entire range, and then select Go To Special, Blanks. This will update your selection to include only the blank cells within the initial selected range. Then set the formula of the first blank cell equal to the cell reference of the cell above—that is, the first account label. Then hit Ctrl+Enter to fill the formula down throughout all selected blank cells. This will set the blank cells equal to the value above it, essentially filling down all of the account labels. Once complete, simply copy/paste special values to replace the formulas with their values.

 **XREF**

Flat data is described in Volume 1, Chapter 16.

## EXAMPLES

Ready to practice? Let's crack open Excel and the sample workbook to get a good feel for conditional summing.

 **PRACTICE**

To work along, please refer to *Conditional Summing Basics.xlsx*.

 **VIDEO**

To watch the solutions video, please visit the Excel University Video Library.

## EXERCISE 1—ONE CONDITION

Let's warm up with something simple: a single-condition SUMIFS function.

 **PRACTICE**

To follow along, please refer to the Exercise 1 worksheet.

In this first exercise, we'll create a report that aggregates data by account. Let's pretend that while our accounting system has many useful built-in reports, there is one specific report that it doesn't provide. Let's also assume that our accounting system can export data to Excel rather easily. Thus we quickly decide that our approach will be to export the data to Excel each period and then use Excel's functions to prepare the needed report.

The desired report structure, by account, is shown in Figure 1 below.

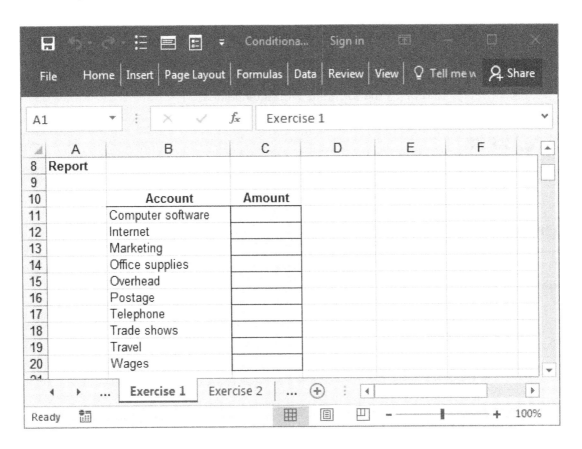

Figure 1

The report's amount values will calculate automatically from the exported data, shown in Figure 2 below.

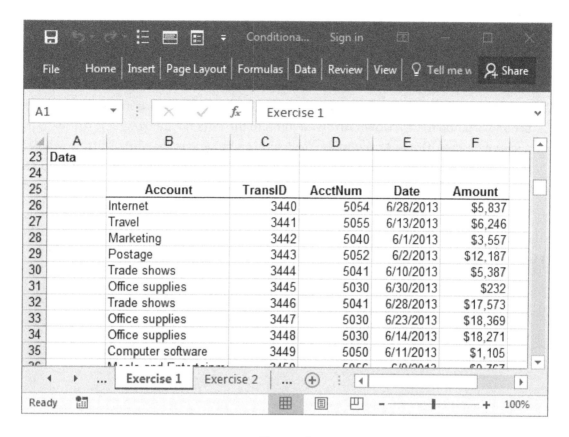

**Figure 2**

To compute the amount column for the report shown in Figure 1, we decide to use the following SUMIFS function for the first account row in the report (cell *C11*):

```
=SUMIFS($F$26:$F$43,$B$26:$B$43,B11)
```

**Where:**

- **$F$26:$F$43** is the column of numbers to add, the amount column.

- **$B$26:$B$43** is the criteria range, the account column.

- **B11** is the value that the criteria range must equal to be included in the function's total.

**KB**

If you want to write the formula by keeping your hands on the keyboard, try these steps. To insert the function, =SUM, Down Arrow to select SUMIFS from the auto-complete list, and Tab to insert the function. To define the first argument, Ctrl+Down Arrow to jump to the data header row, Ctrl+Right Arrow over the amount column, Down Arrow to the first value in the amount column, Ctrl+Shift+Down Arrow to select the amount column, F4 to make the reference absolute, and Comma to begin the next argument. To define the second argument, Ctrl+Down Arrow to jump to the data header row, Left Arrow to the account column, Down Arrow to the first account column value, Ctrl+Shift+Down Arrow to select the account column, F4 to lock down the range reference, and Comma to start the next argument. To define the third argument, Left Arrow to select the report account value. Then close the function with a parenthesis, and hit Enter.

Once the formula is entered, double-click to push the formula down, and bam, we got it! The resulting report is shown in Figure 3 below.

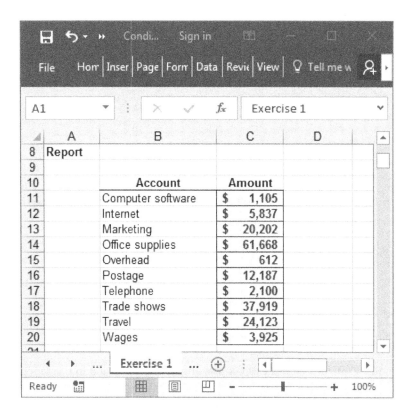

**Figure 3**

**XREF**

The double-click shortcut used to push the formula down is discussed in Volume 1, Chapter 6.

As you can see, the SUMIFS function makes it easy to build this report. However, there is one thing that makes the worksheet unsuitable for recurring-use workbooks and hands-free reporting. The problem is that next month, when we go to update the data, there may be a different number of rows in the export. With our current worksheet design, the report formulas would exclude any additional data rows. This situation could lead to errors and is not very efficient. Can you think of an Excel feature that could help us out? Tables, yes! Our next exercise performs a multiple-condition sum on a table.

 **NOTE**

Technically, this exercise could have been completed with a SUMIF function, since only a single condition was evaluated. My personal preference, however, is to perform all conditional summing work with SUMIFS, as it's easy to add more conditions later. Also, Microsoft reversed the order of the arguments between these two functions, which can be confusing if you are using both functions.

## EXERCISE 2—TWO CONDITIONS

The first exercise was our little warm-up exercise. Now we'll evaluate two conditions using the SUMIFS function to aggregate data stored in a table.

 **PRACTICE**

To practice, please refer to the Exercise 2 worksheet.

This worksheet prepares a summary of selected items and uses the data stored in a table named *tbl_export*. The table contains amount, account, and name columns.

 **DEPENDS ON**

The content in this section depends on knowledge of tables, discussed in Volume 1, Chapter 8.

We will build a report that summarizes the data by account and name, as shown in Figure 4 below.

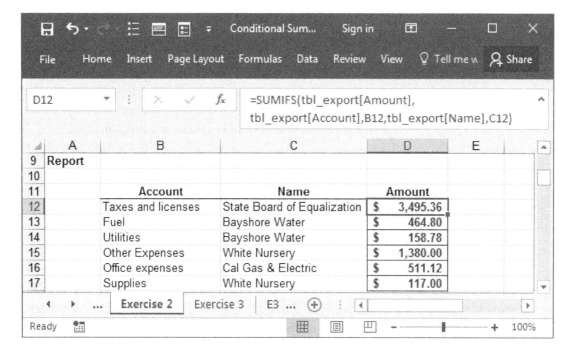

**Figure 4**

Since the first report row is row *12*, the first account criteria value is in *B12*, and the first name criteria value is in *C12*, we would use the following SUMIFS function to populate the first report row:

```
=SUMIFS(tbl_export[Amount],

tbl_export[Account],B12,

tbl_export[Name],C12)
```

**Where:**

- **tbl_export[Amount]** is the column of numbers to add, the amount column.

- **tbl_export[Account]** is the first criteria range, the account column.

- **B12** is the first criteria value.

- **tbl_export[Name]** is the second criteria range, the name column.

- **C12** is the second criteria value.

**KB**

To write the formula with your keyboard, try these steps. To insert the function =SUM, Down Arrow to select SUMIFS, Tab to insert. To define the first argument, tbl, Down Arrow to select the table name from the list, Tab to auto-complete, [ to reveal the structured table reference list, Down Arrow to select Amount, Tab to complete, ], and Comma to begin the next argument. To define the second argument, tbl, Down Arrow to select the table name, Tab to insert, [, Down Arrow to select Account, Tab to insert, ], and Comma. To define the third argument, Left Arrow to select the report account value, and Comma. To define the fourth argument, tbl, Down Arrow to select the table name, Tab, [, Down Arrow to select Name, Tab, ], and Comma. To define the fifth argument, Left Arrow to select the report name value. Type the closing parenthesis, and hit Enter.

Fill the formula down to complete the report. So far so good? Do you love the SUMIFS function? I sure do!

Since we used a table to store the data, and tables automatically expand to include new rows, we can simply paste new transactions into the table and the numbers in the report instantly update. That is the basic idea of hands-free reporting. We'll build on this basic idea throughout this volume.

 **NOTE**

New accounts or names added to the table do not automatically appear in the report, so you'll need to add a new report row and fill the formula into this new row. The need to add new items manually is tolerable if you do not add them very often. If you frequently add new items to the report, then you could consider using a PivotTable, which will automatically adjust to reflect new accounts. PivotTables are covered in Volume 3.

## EXERCISE 3—THREE CONDITIONS

In this exercise, we'll write a conditional summing function that uses three conditions.

 **PRACTICE**

To work along, please refer to the Exercise 3 worksheet.

This exercise is set up similar to the structure I use in the real world. The report is on one worksheet, and the data is stored on its own worksheet. This illustrates the idea of separating the data and the report as discussed in Volume 1.

 **XREF**

Splitting the data from the report is discussed in Volume 1, Chapter 16.

The data is stored in a table named *tbl_qb*. The table contains many columns, four of which are amount, account, name, and type. We want to create a report that aggregates selected items by account, name, and type. The finished report is shown in Figure 5 below.

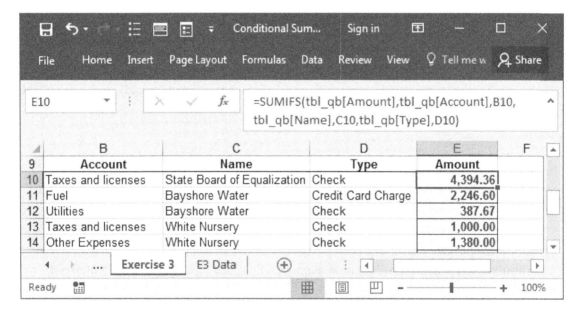

**Figure 5**

We write the following SUMIFS function in cell *E10*, and then fill it down:

```
=SUMIFS(tbl_qb[Amount],

tbl_qb[Account],B10,

tbl_qb[Name],C10,

tbl_qb[Type],D10)
```

**Where:**

- **tbl_qb[Amount]** is the column of numbers to add, the amount column.

- **tbl_qb[Account]** is the first criteria range, the account column.

- **B10** is the first criteria value, the account label in the report.

- **tbl_qb[Name]** is the second criteria range, the name column.

- **C10** is the second criteria value, the name label in the report.

- **tbl_qb[Type]** is the third criteria range, the type column.

- **D10** is the third criteria value, the type label in the report.

We fill the formula down to complete the report. This is the basic SUMIFS usage, and we'll rely on conditional summing frequently throughout the remainder of this text.

## CHAPTER CONCLUSION

I believe that the SUMIFS function is one of Excel's most powerful functions, and I find myself using it all the time. The purpose of this chapter was to introduce conditional summing and cover the basics. We will revisit this function many times in the chapters that follow and greatly expand its utility.

# Chapter 4: Remove Duplicates

## SET UP

When you want to use conditional summing to create a summary report, it sure would be convenient to derive a unique list of the report labels from the underlying data. So, is there an easy way to remove duplicate values from a list? Yes!

To accomplish this goal in older versions of Excel, the Advanced Filter feature could be used. However, beginning with Excel 2007, Microsoft introduced the Remove Duplicates feature, which is a much easier method for deleting duplicate values from a list or a range.

I get the most benefit from this feature when I'm building a summary report from transactional data, and I want a quick way to set up the report labels so that my conditional summing formulas can retrieve the values—for example, a report that sums the amount by account. As you know, I really like to store data on its own worksheet, so I quickly head to the data sheet and select the entire account column and copy it. Then I flip over to the report worksheet and paste the full account column, which will contain many duplicate labels, assuming the source is a transaction listing with many transactions for each account. I remove the duplicate report labels from the pasted account range using the Remove Duplicates feature and then use the SUMIFS function to aggregate the values from the data sheet. This is by far the most common way I personally use the Remove Duplicates feature.

## HOW TO

To remove duplicates from a data range, begin by selecting the entire range or a cell within the range. Next select the Remove Duplicates command as follows:

- Data > Remove Duplicates.

Excel displays the Remove Duplicates dialog box, which allows you to set some options, such as indicating if the data has a header row. Click OK, and Excel will remove duplicate values from the data range and display a confirmation dialog box reporting how many duplicate values were removed and how many unique values remain.

 **NOTE**

> The Remove Duplicates dialog box does not preview the duplicate items that will be deleted. If you want to view duplicate items rather than delete them, use the Conditional Formatting feature to highlight duplicate values.

You may wonder how a duplicate is determined. For our discussion, let's place all data ranges into one of two groups: single column or multicolumn. For simplicity, we'll refer to a single column of data as a list, and we'll refer to a multicolumn range of data as a table.

In a list, a duplicate is a value that appears more than once. Simple.

But in a table—a data region with more than one column—is a duplicate row any row in which one column matches, or must all columns match?

Pretend we have a table that represents a check register and contains columns for check number, date, and amount. Let's say that two rows have the same check number. Are these two rows duplicates? If they have the same check number but different amounts, are they considered duplicates? Excel can apply our definition of duplicate, whatever it may be. If we define duplicate rows as those having the same check numbers, that's no problem. If we define duplicate rows as those in which the check number and amount values are the same, that's fine too. And if we define duplicate rows as those rows in which all three columns must be equal, that's fine too. We tell Excel how we define a duplicate row via the Remove Duplicates dialog box, as shown in Figure 6 below.

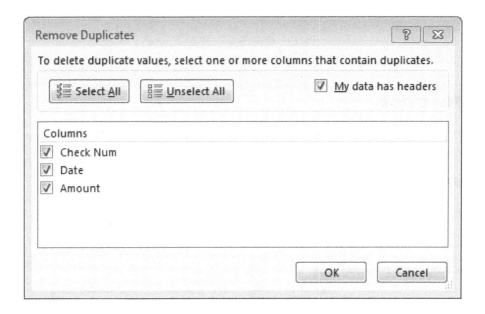

**Figure 6**

We check the columns that must match for the rows to be considered duplicates. If we check all three columns, then all columns must match to be considered a duplicate. If we check a single column, such as Check Num, then Excel only considers that column. If Excel determines that a row is a duplicate, then the whole row is removed (not just the value in the checked box).

 **NOTE**

This feature does not remove all rows that are duplicates; it leaves a unique row. For example, if a list has four rows with the account Cash, the feature will remove three of the four values and leave a single Cash value.

 **XREF**

If you just want to identify the duplicate or unique values, instead of actually removing duplicates, try the Conditional Formatting feature instead, as discussed in Volume 1, Chapter 10.

## EXAMPLES

Let's try a few hands-on exercises at this point.

 **PRACTICE**

To work along, please refer to *Remove Duplicates.xlsx.*

 **VIDEO**

To watch the solutions video, please visit the Excel University Video Library.

## EXERCISE 1—SINGLE COLUMN LIST

In this exercise, we'll remove duplicate values from a single column list.

 **PRACTICE**

To work along, please refer to the Exercise 1 worksheet.

Let's say we have a list of customer IDs with many duplicate values. We want to create a list that contains one cell for each unique customer ID.

We start by selecting any cell in the list, or alternatively, the entire list. Next we select the Remove Duplicates command. From the Remove Duplicates dialog, we select the *My data has headers* checkbox, since our list has a header. Excel removes duplicate values and displays a confirmation dialog box indicating the number of duplicates removed and the number of unique values remaining.

## EXERCISE 2—MULTICOLUMN TABLE

In this exercise, we'll remove duplicates from a table with multiple columns.

 **PRACTICE**

To work along, please refer to the Exercise 2 worksheet.

Here we have a table of check register transactions, and we'd like to remove duplicate rows. We decide that a transaction is a duplicate if all three columns—check num, date, and amount—are equal. If two rows have the same check number but a different date or amount, they are not considered duplicates.

We select any cell in the table or the entire table. Next we select the Remove Duplicates command. We ensure that the *My data has headers* checkbox is selected and that all three columns are checked. Excel removes the duplicates and displays a confirmation dialog box.

## EXERCISE 3—WITH SUMIFS

In this exercise, we'll remove the duplicates from a single column of a table and then use the results to create a report with the SUMIFS function. Sound fun? This is my favorite use of the Remove Duplicates feature and the way that I most frequently use it.

 **PRACTICE**

To work along, please refer to the Exercise 3 worksheet.

We have a big table of transactions that displays checks and related data, as shown in Figure 7 below.

| | A | B | C | D | E | F | G | H | I |
|---|---|---|---|---|---|---|---|---|---|
| 9 | Transactions | | | | | | | | |
| 10 | | | | | | | | | |
| 11 | | CkNum | VID | Vendor | AcctNum | Account | Date | Amount | |
| 12 | | 4241 | SMI333 | Smith Elec | 5020 | Wages | 2/1/2012 | $4,013 | |
| 13 | | 4242 | TRI002 | Trinity Par | 5040 | Marketing | 2/8/2012 | $14,437 | |
| 14 | | 4243 | SSP204 | Switch Su | 5050 | Computer | 2/15/2012 | $17,182 | |
| 15 | | 4244 | TNK900 | Tank Outfi | 5021 | Salary | 2/22/2012 | $14,434 | |
| 16 | | 4245 | SMI333 | Smith Elec | 5056 | Meals and | 2/29/2012 | $96 | |
| 17 | | 4246 | TNK900 | Tank Outfi | 5020 | Wages | 3/7/2012 | $17,801 | |
| 18 | | 4247 | KEY201 | Key Maker | 5020 | Wages | 3/14/2012 | $8,417 | |
| 19 | | 4248 | CCD075 | Cypher Co | 5056 | Meals and | 3/21/2012 | $16,820 | |

**Figure 7**

The VID column contains the vendor ID. We want to generate a report quickly that shows the total amount by vendor.

## SUMMARY

The overall approach is to copy the VID column from the *E3 Data* sheet and paste it into the *Exercise 3* report sheet. Then remove the duplicates from the list on the *Exercise 3* sheet. This will leave one row for each VID. Next write a formula that uses the SUMIFS function to aggregate the transaction data by vendor ID.

## STEP-BY-STEP

Here are the steps for completing the exercise:

**Step 1: Copy the column.** Copy the VID column and paste it into the *Exercise 3* worksheet. The resulting list will contain many duplicate VID values.

**Step 2: Remove duplicates.** Select the VID column on the *Exercise 3* worksheet, and apply the Remove Duplicates command. The resulting list will contain only unique VID values.

**Step 3: Create table.** To make it easier to maintain our workbook over time, and to make it easier to write our report formulas, convert the transaction data range on the *E3 Data* sheet to a table named *tbl_data*.

**Step 4: Formulas.** Finally, use the SUMIFS function to populate the report. Assuming that the first VID value is in *B15*, the following formula works well:

```
=SUMIFS(tbl_data[Amount],tbl_data[VID],B15)
```

**Where:**

- **tbl_data[Amount]** is the column to sum, the amount column.

- **tbl_data[VID]** is the column of the first criteria, the VID column.

- **B15** is the first criteria value, the VID.

You should now have a report on the *Exercise 3* worksheet that summarizes the transactions on the *E3 Data* sheet by VID. I love using the Remove Duplicates feature when building summary reports like this, as I find it to be a very fast approach.

## CHAPTER CONCLUSION

The Remove Duplicates feature is a great companion for the SUMIFS conditional summing function because it provides a quick way to generate the report labels.

# LOOKUPS

*Lookups help us prepare bulletproof, recurring-use workbooks*

# Chapter 5: Lookup Basics

## SET UP

What approach do you use to get a cell value into another cell? To be clear, if you have value in a cell, say a cash value of $100 in cell *B1*, how do you reference that value from another cell? Do you use a direct cell reference, for example =B1? This idea is illustrated in cell *F1* in Figure 8.

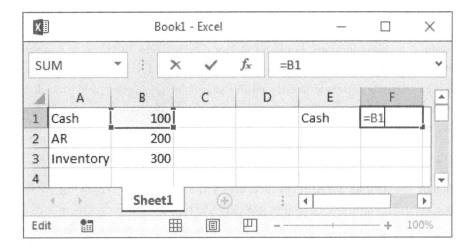

**Figure 8**

The direct cell reference approach is probably the most common way to retrieve the value from a cell. But that approach can lead to errors and inefficiencies, especially in recurring-use workbooks. Let me walk through this idea.

Let's assume that I have a trial balance on a worksheet. My goal is to use selected values from the trial balance in other locations in my workbook, such as in a balance sheet worksheet. If I decide to use simple direct cell references to retrieve the values, the following situations might occur:

- **Sort order.** If I change the sort order of the source range (the trial balance in our example), direct cell references won't keep up with the new sort order. For example, since the report uses *B1* for the cash value, if after the sort the cash value no longer resides in cell *B1*, the references are broken, and the report is inaccurate.

- **New cell locations.** If I update the source range, such as by pasting an updated trial balance, the updated values may occupy different rows than the original values. Cash may no longer reside in *B1*, but since the report continues to use *B1* for cash, the references are broken.

- **Gaps.** What if some items in the source range, such as certain accounts in a trial balance, shouldn't appear on the report? With direct cell references, I wouldn't be able to simply fill the report formula down but would instead have to write unique formulas for each row on the balance sheet. This situation violates the formula consistency principle discussed in Excel University—Volume 1, since you can't write a formula and fill it down. Clearly, this situation is not good.

As you can see, this direct cell reference approach fails to provide bulletproof, recurring-use workbooks.

Fortunately, Microsoft solved these issues years ago, and Excel provides a far better approach for retrieving cell values: lookup functions. Lookup functions are resilient and provide accurate results, even if the sort order changes, new data is pasted in, or gaps occur. Lookup functions help us comply with the formula consistency principle discussed in Volume 1, reduce errors, and provide big efficiency gains. They also have saved me a ton of time over the years, and to me, they are breathtaking.

Now, I can sense that you are not nearly excited enough for our lookup discussion, so let me share a quick story with you.

One of my coaching clients is a CPA firm that prepares a monthly financial reporting package for each of its key clients. The firm exports a handful of QuickBooks reports and copies them into an Excel workbook. Before using lookups, they would copy and paste the correct values from the QB sheets into various report sheets. Sometimes the labels of the QB data and their financials were different, so the firm had to copy and paste each individual cell value. Sometimes multiple lines from QB had to be combined into a single line for the financials, so the firm had to create a formula to add up selected values. The final package included numerous charts and graphs and additional analyses. From start to finish, the process took about forty hours per client per month.

During our Excel coaching sessions, we began to rewire the firm's workbooks, and one of the first things we tackled was efficiently getting the QB values into the financials. We used various Excel lookup functions to populate the financials with the QB values automatically. Now when the firm pastes in updated QB data, the values in the report sheets are automatically updated. The process now takes about four hours per client per month. That's what I'm talking about!

Now are you excited for our discussion? The first lookup function we'll explore is VLOOKUP. If you have never played with the VLOOKUP function, I'm excited for you, as this is one of the cornerstones of performing Excel lookups.

## HOW TO

In essence, the VLOOKUP function finds a match and then returns a related value. Let's say we have a table of transactions, and for each transaction we have an account number, date, and amount, but not an account name, which we want. Fortunately we happen to have handy a list of account numbers with their corresponding account names, called the chart of accounts. We need to write a formula in our transaction table that will look for the account number in the chart of accounts and return the related account name. The VLOOKUP function is perfect for this job, as it finds a match and then returns a related value.

The syntax for the VLOOKUP function is as follows:

```
=VLOOKUP(lookup_value, table_array, col_index_num, [range_
lookup])
```

**Where:**

- **lookup_value** is the value we are trying to find. It is the value that is the "common field" between the two lists. In our example, it is the account number.

- **table_array** is the related table that contains the matching value. In our example, it is the chart of accounts range.

- **col_index_num** is the column that contains the value we want to return. In our case, it is the account name. The value is represented by a relative column number, so if the account name is in the second column, we enter a 2; if the account name is in the fifth column, we enter a 5.

- **[range_lookup]** tells Excel whether or not to perform a range lookup. TRUE performs a range lookup; FALSE does not. This is an optional argument and if omitted defaults to TRUE. A range lookup seeks a match within a range of values, not an exact matching value.

**NOTE**

We will more fully explore the fourth argument, range_lookup, with several exercises below. I find it convenient to think about the argument like this: *true or false, am I doing a range lookup?* The idea of a range lookup will become clear as we work through the exercises.

 **NOTE**

An argument that accepts a TRUE or FALSE value, such as the range_lookup argument, is officially known as a Boolean argument. A Boolean argument can be expressed with TRUE or FALSE values, or with a variety of other values that represent TRUE or FALSE. For example, 0 could be used instead of FALSE. I personally use 0 instead of FALSE, simply because it is one character to enter instead of five. TRUE could be represented by the value of 1 or any other non-zero number. Additionally, the argument could be a cell reference or function that returns a TRUE or FALSE value.

The way I remember these four arguments is by stating the following phrase:

*Go find **this** (argument 1), in **here** (argument 2), and return **this** (argument 3). Am I doing a range lookup (argument 4)?*

## EXAMPLES

Let's work a few hands-on examples to get comfortable writing and implementing the VLOOKUP function.

 **PRACTICE**

To work along, please refer to *Lookup Basics.xlsx.*

 **VIDEO**

To watch the solutions video, please visit the Excel University Video Library.

## EXERCISE 1—BREAKDOWN OF SIMPLE CELL REFERENCES

The purpose of this exercise is to demonstrate how direct cell references fail to provide reliable results over time.

 **PRACTICE**

To follow along, please refer to the Exercise 1 worksheet.

In this exercise, selected account balances have been exported from the accounting system and represent the source data, as shown in Figure 9 below.

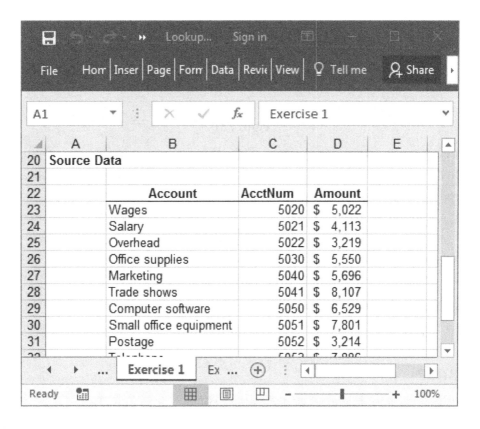

Figure 9

Let's assume we are building a report and need to retrieve selected values from the source data region. We first build the report using formulas containing direct cell references, as shown in Figure 10 below.

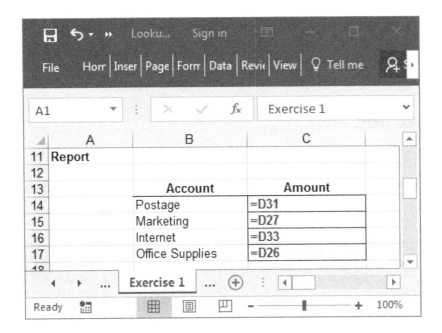

**Figure 10**

Now we want to review the source data, so we sort it in ascending order by account. We then observe the impact of our sort on the accuracy of our report, which is now quite messed up. For example, the value that purports to be postage is actually the value of a different account. This happened because the formula was originally written to retrieve the value in cell *D31*, regardless of what account it represents. Because the direct cell reference formula is static, it didn't automatically rewrite itself to continue to point to the postage account value.

This approach is problematic, as you can see. Do you recall that in Volume 1 the workbook design principles underscored the importance of asking, "How can a user break my workbook?" In our example, a user will unintentionally break the workbook by simply sorting the source range.

 **XREF**

Workbook design principles are discussed in Volume 1, Chapter 19.

Before we move on to our preferred approach, I want to point out some subtle issues. In the report above, each formula that pulls the amount value from the source data region is unique and was written for a specific cell in the report. This is inefficient and can result in errors.

Since a custom formula was used for each cell, the workbook takes longer to set up and maintain on an ongoing basis. This is inefficient. If consistent formulas are used instead, one formula can be quickly filled down throughout all cells in the report.

 **XREF**

The concept of using consistent formulas in a range is discussed in Volume 1, Chapter 16.

This approach also leads to potential errors because next month, when we paste new data into the source data region, the accounts may not fall into the same rows as last month. This increases the likelihood of errors, because the report formulas may retrieve the wrong values.

This exercise tries to demonstrate why the direct cell reference approach is inefficient and error prone. Let's try building the report again, this time using a lookup function.

## EXERCISE 2—ACCOUNT VALUES

In this exercise, we'll populate the report from Exercise 1 using the VLOOKUP function.

 **PRACTICE**

To work along, please refer to the Exercise 2 worksheet.

Since the approach demonstrated in Exercise 1 is unreliable, let's try using the VLOOKUP function. We write the following formula in the first cell in the report:

=VLOOKUP(B14,$B$23:$D$35,3,FALSE)

**Where:**

- **B14** is the value we are looking up, the account name. Note the use of a relative reference so that as we fill the formula down, the function will operate on the proper account name in each row.

- **$B$23:$D$35** is the range in which we are looking, the source data region. Note the use of absolute cell references so that as we fill the formula down, the function will continue to operate on this region.

- **3** is the column that contains the value we wish to return, the amount column.

- **FALSE** means we are not performing a range lookup.

**KB**

To write the formula with the keyboard, try these steps: =VL, and then Tab to insert VLOOKUP. To define the first argument, Left Arrow to select the first report account value, and then Comma. To define the second argument, Ctrl+Down Arrow to jump down to the data header row, Left Arrow then Down Arrow to select the first account value, Ctrl+Shift+Down to select the account column, Ctrl+Shift+Right to extend the selection to include the whole data range, F4, and Comma. To define the third argument, enter 3 and then Comma. To define the fourth argument, Down Arrow to select FALSE, and Tab to insert it. Type a closing parenthesis and Enter.

After the formula is written, we can fill it down and watch with joy as our report values are retrieved.

The best part is that the report remains accurate even if the order of the source data changes. Go ahead and resort the source data region and watch as the VLOOKUP function continues to return accurate results. Next month when we paste new data into the source data region, the VLOOKUP will return accurate results even if the account order is different.

Because the report formulas are consistent, we can update the top formula in the range and then fill it down, making it fast and easy to maintain the report over time.

That was our little warm-up exercise. Now that we have covered the basics, let's dig into many additional exercises to explore the VLOOKUP function more fully.

## EXERCISE 3—WITH NAMED RANGES

In this exercise, we'll use the VLOOKUP function to find the account name associated with the account number.

 **PRACTICE**

To work along, please refer to the Exercise 3 worksheet.

In the world in which we live, ID/label pairs are all around us and permeate the accounting systems and other applications that we use. What is an ID/label pair? Things like a department number and a department name; customer number, customer name; item number, item name; and so forth.

You probably work with ID/label pairs all the time and sometimes may receive a data extract that has the ID but not the corresponding label. In this exercise, we'll use an ID/label pair that is sure to be familiar: the account number and account name pair, commonly referred to as the chart of accounts.

Did you notice in the previous exercise that we needed to lock down the second argument by making the range reference absolute? Since we filled the formula down, we had to lock down the range reference so it did not change as the formula was filled. This function often requires an absolute reference for the second argument. Let's name the lookup range in this exercise so that we don't need to expressly use dollar signs to create the absolute reference.

 **DEPENDS ON**

The mechanics for how to define a name is discussed in Volume 1, Chapter 7.

In this worksheet, we use our company's chart of accounts, a partial copy of which is shown in Figure 11 below.

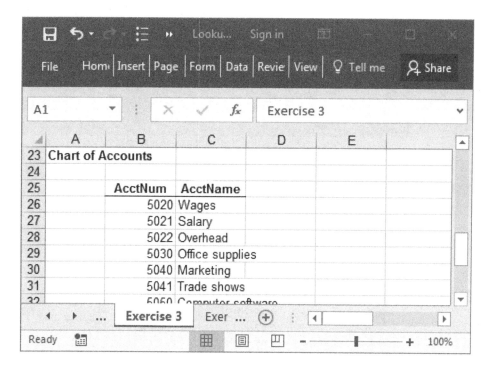

**Figure 11**

Since we know that we'll ultimately use this range as the source for a lookup function, we decide to name it *coa*, short for chart of accounts.

Let's say we've pasted an extract from our accounting system into Excel and that it contains various transactions. The problem is that the extract contains the account number only, and not the account name, so we need to populate the transactions with the proper account name. Since the first account number is stored in *C12*, we write the following formula and fill it down, the results of which are shown in Figure 12 below.

```
=VLOOKUP(C12,coa,2,0)
```

**Where:**

- **C12** is the value we are looking up, the account number.

- **coa** is the lookup range, the name that references the chart of accounts.

- **2** is the column that contains the value we want to return, the account name.

- **0** means we are not performing a range lookup. This Boolean argument accepts TRUE or FALSE, but this can be expressed in several ways, including 0 for FALSE and any other number for TRUE.

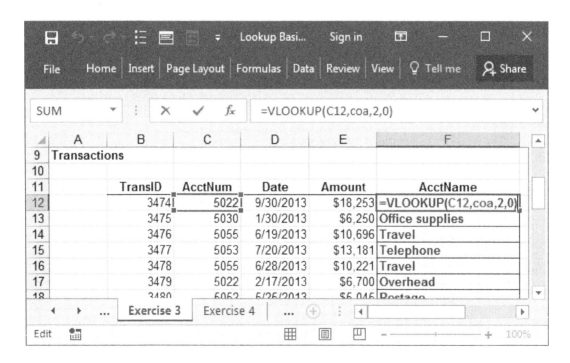

Figure 12

The VLOOKUP function looks up the account number in the chart of accounts and returns the corresponding account name. We named the chart of accounts range *coa*, which offers several benefits. Most obviously, we don't need to fiddle with locking down the range reference with dollar signs to make the reference absolute. More importantly, it is now very easy to write lookup functions throughout the workbook because we can quickly type *coa* for the second argument and don't need to browse to the range and select it with our mouse. It feels faster and more accurate to use the name. Additionally, we get all of the other standard benefits of names, including quick navigation, as described in detail in Volume 1.

So far so good? Now, here is a question for you: does this worksheet violate any of our workbook design principles?

It does. It violates at least two of the workbook design principles discussed in Volume 1. Namely, it is not bulletproof, because a user can unintentionally break it, and it is not efficient to maintain on an ongoing basis.

Let me clarify with a question. If a user adds a new account under the chart of accounts, will that new account automatically be included in the formula? No, it will not. Even though we are using a named reference, the name will not automatically expand to include the new account if the account is entered under the range. Since we didn't anticipate and address this issue up front, our workbook is not bulletproof.

Here's another question for you: is this worksheet efficient to maintain on an ongoing basis? No, it is not. It is a hassle to add a new account under the chart of accounts, because when we do, we need to go in and modify the name *coa* to include the new account. This is a slow way to make updates. Now that we understand these design issues with the worksheet, let's address them in the next exercise.

 **NOTE**

If you add a new account by inserting a row within the range, then the name expands to include the new account. However, if you type a new value *under* the named range, the name does not expand to include the new account.

## EXERCISE 4—WITH SKINNY ROW

In this exercise, we'll use the Skinny Row Technique.

 **PRACTICE**

To work along, please refer to the Exercise 4 worksheet.

As a reminder, the Skinny Row Technique discussed in Volume 1 helps reduce the likelihood of errors and improves efficiency. Here we'll create a skinny row under the last account and then include the skinny row in our named range. The skinny row provides a visual boundary and reminder to insert new account rows above it. Since the name includes the skinny row, rows inserted above the skinny row will automatically be included in the name and thus in the lookup formulas.

### DEPENDS ON

The mechanics for implementing the Skinny Row Technique is discussed in Volume 1, Chapter 12.

In our worksheet, we add a skinny row under the chart of accounts. Then we name the chart of accounts range, including the skinny row, *accounts*. Then we write the following formula:

```
=VLOOKUP(C12,accounts,2,0)
```

**Where:**

- **C12** is the value we are looking up, the account number.

- **accounts** is the lookup range, the name that references the chart of accounts.

- **2** is the column that contains the value we wish to return, the account name.

- **0** means we are not performing a range lookup.

Since the chart of accounts now has a skinny row underneath it, and since the name *accounts* includes the skinny row, the worksheet is easy to maintain over time.

An approach I prefer even more than skinny rows is tables. Let's play with this approach with a hands-on exercise.

## EXERCISE 5—WITH TABLES

In this exercise, we'll use a VLOOKUP function to retrieve a related value from a table.

### PRACTICE

To work along, please refer to the Exercise 5 worksheet.

We have a customer master list that contains the customer ID, name, and state. We are working with a data extract of transactions from our accounting system that contains the customer ID, date, and amount. Since we need each transaction row also to reflect the customer name and state, we decide to use VLOOKUP.

Because we will use this workbook on a recurring basis and paste in updated customer lists from time to time, we decide to use a table to store the customer list. The table will automatically expand to include any new customers.

 **DEPENDS ON**

Tables are discussed in detail in Volume 1, Chapter 8.

First, we convert the customer list to a table named ***tbl_customers***. Next we write the formulas to pull the customer name and customer state values from ***tbl_customers*** into our transaction list based on the customer ID, as shown in Figure 13.

In the transaction list, cell ***B11*** stores the customer ID for the first row, so we write the following formula to populate the customer name column:

    =VLOOKUP(B11,tbl_customers,2,0)

**Where:**

- **B11** is the value we are looking up, the customer ID.

- **tbl_customers** is the lookup range, the customer list.

- **2** is the column that contains the value we wish to return, the customer name.

- **0** means we are not performing a range lookup.

Next we write a similar formula to populate the customer state column:

    =VLOOKUP(B11,tbl_customers,3,0)

**Where:**

- **B11** is the value we are looking up, the customer ID.

- **tbl_customers** is the lookup range, the customer list.

- **3** is the column that contains the value we wish to return, the customer state.

- **0** means we are not performing a range lookup.

After filling both formulas down, we are done, and our report is complete, as shown in Figure 13 below.

| | CustID | Date | Amount | Cust Name | Cust State |
|---|---|---|---|---|---|
| 9 | Transactions | | | | |
| 11 | POL412 | 5/4/2013 | $ 821 | Polaris Enterprises | ID |
| 12 | LHC001 | 7/3/2013 | $ 12,336 | Electron LHC | TX |
| 13 | EBD220 | 9/21/2013 | $ 15,051 | Entangled By Design | WI |
| 14 | RAM101 | 8/28/2013 | $ 13,966 | Ramsey Electronics | CA |
| 15 | QEX711 | 3/15/2013 | $ 9,737 | Quark Express | SD |
| 16 | DIG290 | 5/1/2013 | $ 4,423 | Digital Media, Inc. | AZ |
| 17 | POL412 | 7/10/2013 | $ 16,311 | Polaris Enterprises | ID |
| 18 | NEW011 | 9/9/2013 | $ 6,..5 | Newton Apples | MI |

**Figure 13**

My favorite part about this exercise is that it illustrates a powerful and reliable system you can apply often. Store the underlying data in a table, and then use the table's name in your lookup formulas. Since the table will auto-expand as new data is added, and since the formulas use the table's name, you know that new data will automatically be included in the formulas. This approach will no doubt improve efficiency and reduce errors in recurring-use workbooks.

Are you good? If so, let's keep going.

## EXERCISE 6—DEPARTMENT DATA VALIDATION

We want to allow a user to enter a department number and have Excel automatically populate the related department name. The result is illustrated in Figure 14 below.

 **PRACTICE**

To work along, please refer to the Exercise 6 worksheet.

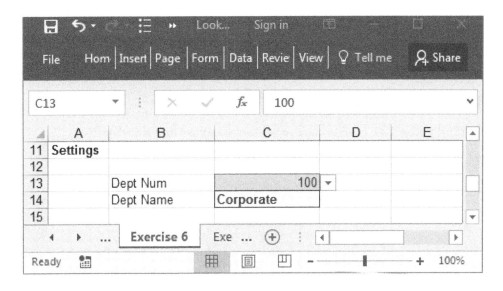

**Figure 14**

## SUMMARY

If we think about the goal for a minute, we can piece together the Excel items needed. Here we'll discuss the features and functions required at a summary level, and in the Step-by-Step section below we'll chronologically work through the detailed steps.

We allow the user to enter a department number into the input cell and then use the VLOOKUP function to retrieve the proper department name.

Since we are asking Excel to perform a lookup, we'll need to store the department list somewhere inside the workbook. Since we want the user's experience to be clean, we place the department list on a separate worksheet. Since we may ultimately add more departments over time, we choose to store the department list in a table named *tbl_depts*.

Since we want to be clear about which cell requires input, we identify the input cell with the Input cell style.

Since our lookup formula is designed to return the name for the departments appearing in our list, it would return an error if the user entered a department number that wasn't in the list. To prevent this error, we provide a drop-down to restrict input to a list of valid department numbers with the data validation feature.

Since data validation does not directly support structured table references, we must first set up the custom name *dd_depts,* which refers to the structured table reference for the department number column.

Here is a summary of the independent Excel items discussed above:

- A **table** stores the department list.

- The **named reference** enables the drop-down list to use the table data.

- The **Input cell style** highlights the input cell.

- The **data validation** feature provides the in-cell drop-down.

- The **VLOOKUP** function retrieves the department name.

Good times! Now that we have worked through the overall concepts, let's sort through the specifics.


## STEP-BY-STEP

Here are the steps to setting up the worksheet.

 **DEPENDS ON**

This exercise depends on knowledge of tables (Volume 1, Chapter 8), named references (Volume 1, Chapter 7), data validation (Volume 1, Chapter 9), and input cells (Volume 1, Chapter 14).

**Step 1: Table.** Since we use the workbook on a recurring basis and want to make it easy to add new departments, we convert the ordinary range of departments found on the *Exercise 6 Data* sheet to a table named *tbl_depts*.

 **NOTE**

My personal preference is to start table names with tbl_.

**Step 2: Named range.** We need to set up a name that refers to the table's department number column so that we can use it with the data validation feature. We assign the name *dd_depts* to the department number column of the table *tbl_depts[Dept Num]*.

 **NOTE**

My personal preference is to start names that are used to provide a drop-down list with dd_.

**Step 3: Input cell style.** We want to make it easy for the user to identify which cell requires input, so we apply the Input cell style to the input cell.

**Step 4: Data validation.** We create an in-cell drop-down in the input cell by setting up data validation to allow a list equal to our name *dd_depts*.

**Step 5: Lookup formula.** After the user picks a valid department number from the drop-down list in *C13*, we ask Excel to display the corresponding department name with the following lookup function:

```
=VLOOKUP(C13,tbl_depts,2,0)
```

**Where:**

- **C13** is the value we are looking up, the department number.

- **tbl_depts** is the lookup range, the table of departments.

- **2** is the column that has the value we wish to return, the department name column.

- **0** means we are not doing a range lookup.

Wow, wasn't that a rush? Using five independent Excel features and functions in harmony to achieve a goal—so fun!

This specific combination of features and functions is quite handy. Once comfortable coordinating the individual steps, you'll quickly be able to use this approach in your workbooks.

## EXERCISE 7—BALANCE SHEET LOOKUP

In this exercise we'll build a financial statement from an export from our accounting system. We'll set up the workbook so that each period when we paste in updated data, Excel automatically recalculates the financial statement amounts. Each period, we just paste and go; that's hands-free reporting.

 **PRACTICE**

To work along, please reference the Exercise 7 worksheet.

Let's pretend that periodically we obtain an extract from our accounting system that reflects each account's current balance. For simplicity, we'll refer to our export as the trial balance. Let's also pretend we want Excel to automatically place the values found in the trial balance into a perfectly formatted financial statement.

The overall idea is simple: create one worksheet in the workbook dedicated to storing the trial balance, and then set up the financial statement using lookup formulas that pull the right values into the right cells in the report. Since the report values are generated by formulas, they will automatically refresh as soon as an updated trial balance is pasted into the workbook.

You've already written many VLOOKUP functions, so this should be pretty easy. I did add one little twist, which demonstrates how to use column-only references with a lookup formula.

 **NOTE**

How can we ensure that all data in the trial balance flows properly through to the financial statement? With an ErrorCk sheet, of course.

 **XREF**

The error check concept is introduced in Volume 1, Chapter 15, and is discussed further in Chapter 25: Improve Error Check with Boolean Values and the AND Function.

Take a look at the *Exercise 7 Data* sheet to observe the exported data. These are the values we'll ultimately pull into the *Exercise 7* sheet, which represents the balance sheet. We'll use the VLOOKUP function to retrieve the values.

We want to write our balance sheet formulas so that they include any new rows that may appear in the trial balance over time. My preferred method is to store the trial balance in a table. Since this isn't always an available option or is sometimes not appropriate, let's explore an alternative method: column-only references.

A column-only reference, such as *B:B*, includes the entire column. If next month's data occupies more rows than last month, using a column-only reference as an argument ensures the function will include all data.

 **XREF**

Column-only references are introduced in Volume 1, Chapter 3. This exercise illustrates a practical application of them.

The lookup formula used to pull the values from the trial balance into the balance sheet follows:

```
=VLOOKUP(B14, 'Exercise 7 Data'!B:C,2,0)
```

**Where:**

- **B14** is the value we are looking up, the account name.

- **'Exercise 7 Data'!B:C** is the lookup range, the exported data on the *Exercise 7 Data* sheet; note the column-only reference *B:C*.

- **2** is the column that contains the value we want to return, the amount.

- **0** means we are not doing a range lookup.

**KB**

Here are the steps to writing the formula using only your keyboard. Type =VL, and then hit Tab to insert the VLOOKUP function from the auto-complete list into the cell. Left Arrow twice to insert the **B14** cell reference into the first function argument. Type a comma to finish the first argument. Use Ctrl+PageDown to switch to the **Exercise 7 Data** sheet. Use the arrow keys to navigate to any cell in column **B**. Hit Ctrl+Space to select the entire column. Hold down Shift and then press the Right Arrow to extend your selection to include column **C** as well. Type a comma to finish the second argument. Type a 2 as the third argument, and then a comma. Type 0, close the parenthesis, and then press Enter.

The results are shown in the partial balance sheet in Figure 15 below.

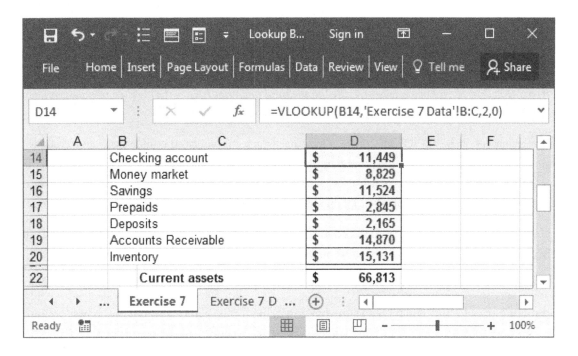

**Figure 15**

**XREF**

Please note that this exercise worksheet relies on the SUBTOTAL function for adding and utilizes skinny rows. These topics are discussed in Volume 1, Chapters 11 and 12, respectively.

Since the report was built with formulas, when we paste in the updated trial balance next month, the balance sheet amounts refresh *automagically*!

## TRICK QUESTIONS

Okay, time for a quick intermission between our hands-on exercises. I'd like to ask you some trick questions about the VLOOKUP function.

**Question #1:** *Where does it look?*

When the VLOOKUP function is trying to find the matching value in the lookup range (as specified by the second argument), where within that range is it actually looking? I'll give you two choices: it looks in all cells of the lookup range, or it looks only in the first column. What do you think?

**Answer:** The VLOOKUP function looks for a matching value in the first column of the lookup range—that is, the left-most column within the range defined by the second argument. After a match is found, the VLOOKUP then uses the other columns in the range to return its result. But the original match is performed within the first column only.

**Question #2:** *Does the column number specified in the third argument refer to the absolute worksheet column or the relative column within the lookup range?*

The third argument of the VLOOKUP function indicates which column has the value we want to return. This argument is specified as a column index number, such as 5, 7, or 9. So the question is whether the column index number refers to the absolute worksheet column—such as column B = 2 and column E = 5—or does it refer to the relative column within the lookup range, as defined in the second argument? What do you think?

**Answer:** The column number refers to the relative column within the lookup range. So if the amount column is the second column within the lookup range, but happens to be in column E, we would use a value of 2.

**Question #3:** *What happens if a matching value can't be found?*

If the function tries to find a matching value, but a matching value can't be found in the first column of the lookup range, what happens? I'll give you two choices: Excel returns an error code, or Excel returns the closest match. What do you think?

**Answer**: It depends on the value of the fourth argument. If the fourth argument is FALSE, then the function returns the error code #N/A when a matching value is not found. If the fourth argument is TRUE, then it returns the closest match based on the function's range lookup logic.

The range lookup logic tells the function to search row by row, one at a time, in order, until it finds a row that contains a value that is less than the lookup value and where the next row is greater than the lookup value. At this point, the function stops looking and returns the related value. According to the Excel help file, "The next largest value that is less than lookup_value is returned." This logic is, admittedly, very confusing. It reminds me of the show *The Price is Right*, where the contestants need to guess the highest price without going over. It is easier to make sense of this logic when applied in an actual worksheet, so we'll do some additional exercises shortly that will help.

**Question #4:** *Does the underlying data in the lookup range need to be sorted?*

Does the lookup range, as defined by the second argument, need to be sorted in any particular order for the function to return an accurate result? Or can the data in the lookup range be unsorted? So, what do you think?

**Answer**: It depends on the value of the fourth argument. If it is TRUE, the data must be sorted in ascending order by the first column. If it is FALSE, the underlying data can be unsorted.

 **NOTE**

> The sort order issue often triggers errors in VLOOKUP results. When you get unexpected results from a VLOOKUP function, be sure to check the fourth argument. If it is TRUE, sort the data. If a range lookup is not needed, set the fourth argument to FALSE.

Speaking of that fourth argument, we haven't really played with it yet. In the exercises thus far, we've used FALSE or 0. I think it is time we use TRUE to perform some range lookups.

## RANGE LOOKUPS

Earlier, when describing the fourth argument of the VLOOKUP function, I recommended thinking about the argument by asking a question: true or false, am I doing a range lookup? Before we jump into the following exercises, let's take a moment to understand the meaning of the term *range lookup*.

In the context of the VLOOKUP function, think of a range as values between a starting point and an ending point, not as a worksheet range. A simple example is the range of numbers from 100 to 199, which is a single range of values.

An example of multiple ranges is 100 to 199, 200 to 499, and 500 to 999. Multiple ranges are often stored in an Excel worksheet stacked up, in a table structure. Typically, the range beginning and ending points are stored in columns with labels such as From and To, or Start and End. This idea is illustrated in Table 2 below.

| Account From | Account To | Label |
|---|---|---|
| 100 | 199 | Sales |
| 200 | 499 | Cost of Sales |
| 500 | 999 | SG&A |

Table 2

With a range lookup, we are trying to match a value within a range. For example, we are trying to figure out the financial statement label for account number 222. To figure this out, we could examine Table 2 and see which range account 222 falls within. It looks like account 222 falls with the range of 200 to 499 and thus has the Cost of Sales label.

Let's work through several exercises now so that you are comfortable performing range lookups and can implement them in your workbooks.

 **NOTE**

I need to clarify one detail that is sometimes confusing. Microsoft chose Exact Match and Approximate Match as the descriptions for the two choices for the fourth argument. These descriptions often mislead people. Approximate Match implies that when the values have similar, but not exact, letters or words, or when the lookup value has extra trailing spaces or contains abbreviations, Excel will make the match. Thinking about it in these terms, with text strings in mind, may yield incorrect results.

It is more helpful to think about Approximate Match in terms of numeric values. Approximate Match indicates that the lookup range values do not need to match the exact value in the worksheet, which is precisely what we saw when we located account 222 in Table 2 above.

I disregard Microsoft's descriptions and prefer to think of the fourth argument like this: true or false, am I doing a range lookup? Thinking of the fourth argument in these terms will keep you on track.

If you need to perform a fuzzy lookup, where text strings have similar, but not exact, letters and words, trailing spaces, or abbreviations, please feel free to check out the free Microsoft add-in named Fuzzy Lookup Add-In for Excel, downloadable from the Microsoft.com website.

## EXERCISE 8—BONUS RANGE LOOKUP

In this exercise, we'll perform a simple range lookup.

 **PRACTICE**

To work along, please refer to the Exercise 8 worksheet.

Each quarter, bonuses are awarded to sales managers based on sales performance. Sales between $0 and $9,999 earn $0 bonus, sales between $10,000 and $49,999 earn a $1,000 bonus, and sales between $50,000 and $99,999 earn a $2,500 bonus.

The bonus amount can easily be determined for any given sales amount by doing a range lookup. The VLOOKUP function performs range lookups very efficiently, and thus we'll enlist this incredible function to find our bonus amount.

We start by setting up an input cell so the user can enter the sales amount. We apply the Input cell style to identify the cell *C13*.

Next we set up the bonus table and name it *tbl_bonus*.

Finally, we write the lookup formula:

```
=VLOOKUP(C13,tbl_bonus,3,TRUE)
```

**Where:**

- **C13** is the value we are looking up, the sales amount.

- **tbl_bonus** is the lookup range, the bonus table.

- **3** is the column that has the value we want to return, the bonus amount.

- **TRUE** means we are performing a range lookup.

The worksheet at this stage appears in Figure 16 below.

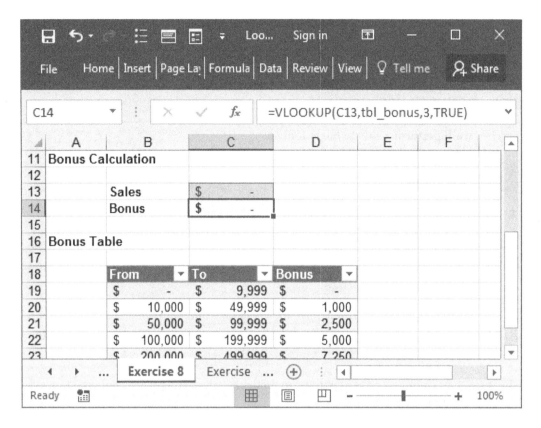

**Figure 16**

A user can now enter a sales amount, and the VLOOKUP function will return the proper bonus amount. Go ahead and give it a try. Enter a few different sales values, and confirm that the bonus amount is properly retrieved. Try it right now.

If you enter a negative sales amount, the value will not be found in the bonus table, and thus the VLOOKUP function will return an error. To prevent this situation, we have a few options. One option is to update the formula to trap the error and display an alternative result. Another option is to add additional values to the table. A third option is to restrict entry. Can you think of an Excel feature that we could use to limit entry to a positive number? If you said "Data validation," then good for you. So, let's turn on data validation for the input cell and allow a decimal number greater than or equal to zero.

 **XREF**

Trapping the error and displaying an alternative result can be accomplished with the IFERROR function, which is discussed in Chapter 9: Trap Errors with IFERROR.

Now, just to be sure you have a full understanding of the way this works, I'll ask a couple of trick questions.

**Question:** *Does the bonus table have to be sorted?*

**Answer:** Yes, the bonus table must be sorted in ascending order for the function to return an accurate result. This is because the forth argument is TRUE, and we are doing a range lookup. The data must be sorted by the lookup column, which as you know is the first column in the lookup range.

**Question:** *Does the VLOOKUP function need the To column to operate properly?*

**Answer:** No, it is not needed. Go ahead and delete the contents of the To column by highlighting the cells and pressing Delete on your keyboard. Now enter various sales amounts and confirm that the VLOOKUP function continues to return accurate results. At first, this can be a funny sensation.

As we discussed earlier, the VLOOKUP function examines only the first column in the lookup range when performing its match. That means we need only the From column. All other columns, including the To column, are ignored during the matching process. Even though Excel needs only the From column, we humans love to see the From and To columns. For some reason, seeing both sides provides comfort.

The fact that Excel considers only the From column during its match explains why the function will return a bonus amount, even if you enter a sales amount that is greater than the last value in the To column, or $999,999. That is, if you enter a sales amount of $1,000,000 or more, the function will continue to return $10,000 for the bonus amount. This is because only the first column in the lookup range is considered when the VLOOKUP performs its match.

## EXERCISE 9—DATE RANGE LOOKUPS

The ability to perform range lookups often comes in handy—for example, when you need to match dates. What? Can we do range lookups with dates? You bet.

 **PRACTICE**

To work along, please refer to the Exercise 9 worksheet.

Assume we have a list of transactions, and each record has a date. We can find the date in a range and then return a related value. Some examples include looking up the date to find the historical stock closing price, looking up the date to determine the proper sales tax rate, and looking up the date to return a label such as a fiscal quarter label.

In this exercise, we'll look up a date to find the appropriate quarter label. Our company runs on a 6/30 fiscal year end. Since Excel features are designed around a traditional calendar year, we need a convenient way to remap the actual transaction dates into the periods our company needs, which are fiscal quarters. For our company, the three months ending 9/30 is Q1, and the three month ending 12/31 is Q2, and so on through Q4, which ends on 6/30. It is easy to set up a table that translates these date ranges into quarter labels, an example of which is shown in Figure 17 below.

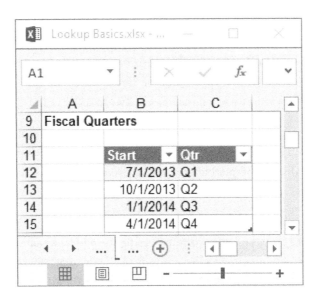

**Figure 17**

We could have easily included a quarter end column, so that we could see both the start and end dates of each quarter, and that would have been just fine. Since the VLOOKUP function looks only in the first column of the lookup range, we'll leave it out; it is not needed by Excel.

If you are working along, the first step will be to convert the quarter lookup range into a table named *tbl_qtrs*. Next use the VLOOKUP function to retrieve the correct fiscal label. Assuming the first transaction date is stored in *C21*, the following formula should do the trick:

```
=VLOOKUP(C21,tbl_qtrs,2,TRUE)
```

**Where:**

- **C21** is the value we are looking up, the transaction date.

- **tbl_qtrs** is the lookup range, the quarter table.

- **2** is the column that contains the value we wish to return, the quarter label.

- **TRUE** tells Excel we are doing a range lookup.

Fill the formula down to complete the worksheet, as shown in Figure 18 below.

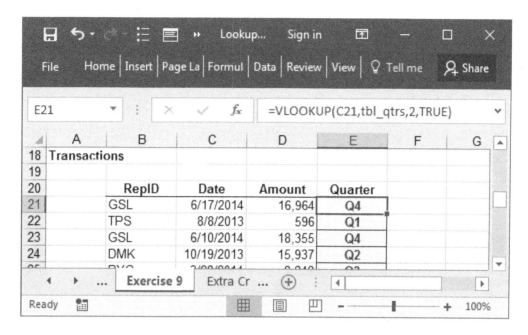

**Figure 18**

Once you have assigned fiscal quarter labels to all transactions, it is a simple matter to write formulas that compute quarter totals. Can you think of how? Come on, be there for me. What function could we use? If you said SUMIFS, I'm proud of you! We could also use a PivotTable, but that is a feature we are saving for a future volume.

## CHAPTER CONCLUSION

My wife and I have three school-aged children, and every Thursday night we take self-defense classes. I admire our *sensei* for his training methods. I've learned from him that repetition is key when learning a new self-defense maneuver. In fact, he has a saying: drill for skill. Each defense maneuver is practiced over and over so our bodies and minds memorize it. Eventually the skill becomes second nature.

In this chapter, we used the VLOOKUP function in nine different exercises. My goal is that you can comfortably use the function and understand its subtle details. Mastery of this function is a critical Excel skill.

It almost seems that the VLOOKUP function has become an indicator of your Excel skill level. A question often posed when trying to assess a user's proficiency is "Do you know VLOOKUP?" It is my goal that you thoroughly understand and embrace this function and use it in your workbooks. I hope that by doing so, you'll be able to complete your job tasks more efficiently.

# Chapter 6: Improve VLOOKUP with MATCH

## SET UP

As incredible as the VLOOKUP function is, it does have limitations. Experienced VLOOKUP users know what I'm talking about.

 **DEPENDS ON**

> The content in this chapter depends on the VLOOKUP discussion in Chapter 5: Lookup Basics.

Long-time VLOOKUP users often lament about three limitations:

- The fixed third argument.

- Text vs. numeric values.

- Can't go left.

In this chapter, we'll discuss the fixed third-argument limitation, while we'll address the other limitations and related workarounds in subsequent chapters.

## THE FIXED THIRD ARGUMENT

The third argument to the VLOOKUP function allows us to identify which column contains the value to return. For example, if we wanted to return the customer name value, and customer name is stored in the fifth column, then we enter a 5 for this argument. If the customer name is in column 9, we enter 9, and so on. The problem we encounter is when a new column is inserted between the lookup column (column 1) and the return column specified in the third argument. Most functions automatically update their arguments and continue to work when you insert a new column.

However, what is curious about the VLOOKUP function is that it does not automatically update its third argument to adjust for new columns inserted between the lookup column and the return column. Isn't that strange? I think so. I believe this limitation exists because the third argument is expressed as an integer rather than as a range reference, and Excel leaves the integer as a static value. This limitation has caught me off guard and created errors and inefficiencies in my workbooks. This is why I use the MATCH workaround, discussed at length below.

## HOW TO

We first must understand the MATCH function before we can use it to work around the VLOOKUP limitation.

The MATCH function returns the relative position of an item in a list. It may take a moment for this to settle in. Perhaps close your eyes and think about this for a moment:

*The MATCH function returns the relative position of an item in a list.*

Can you visualize that yet?

If I had a list of month abbreviations in a worksheet, and I asked Excel to MATCH Jan, then the MATCH function would return 1 because Jan is in the first position of the list. If Excel matched Jun, then the function would return 6, because Jun is in the sixth position in the list. Got it? MATCH returns the relative position of an item in a vertical or horizontal list.

Here is the syntax for the MATCH function:

```
=MATCH(lookup_value, lookup_array, [match_type])
```

**Where:**

- **lookup_value** is the value you are trying to find—for example, Jan.

- **lookup_array** is the range in which you are looking—for example, the list of month abbreviations.

- **[match_type]** is an optional argument that specifies the type of match to perform; we'll mostly use 0 to indicate exact match. Other options include 1 for less than and -1 for greater than. For all exercises in this volume, we'll use 0 because we want an exact match. Check out Excel's help system for additional information.

We'll practice the MATCH function in our first exercise below, but before we get started with the exercise, let's talk about how the function can be used to work around the VLOOKUP limitation. Each time we wrote a VLOOKUP function in Chapter 5: Lookup Basics, we entered an integer value for the third argument. When we wanted to return the value from the second column, we entered 2; when we wanted to return the value from the fourth column, we entered 4.

In this chapter, rather than use a static value as the third argument, we will use a MATCH function. The nested MATCH function will determine the proper column number and return it to the VLOOKUP function. As you know, the MATCH function returns the relative position number of an item in a list. We ask it to return the relative column position based on the column labels. The relative column number is returned to the VLOOKUP function, creating a dynamic third argument. By nesting the MATCH function inside the VLOOKUP, we enable the VLOOKUP function to adapt easily to newly inserted columns.

 **DEPENDS ON**

Nested functions are discussed in Volume 1, Chapter 17.

Let's take it one step at a time and start with the MATCH function. Crack open the exercise workbook and be sure to work along.

## EXAMPLES

Let's work through some hands-on exercises.

 **PRACTICE**

To work along, please refer to *Match.xlsx.*

 **VIDEO**

To watch the solutions video, please visit the Excel University Video Library.

# EXERCISE 1—MATCH

In this exercise, we'll use the MATCH function to return the relative position number of an item in a list.

 **PRACTICE**

To work along, please refer to the Exercise 1 worksheet.

In our first baby warm-up exercise, we'll discover exactly what the MATCH function does and the value it returns.

We want the user to pick a month from a drop-down list and then have the MATCH function return the relative position number of the month from a list of months.

The idea is illustrated in Figure 19 below.

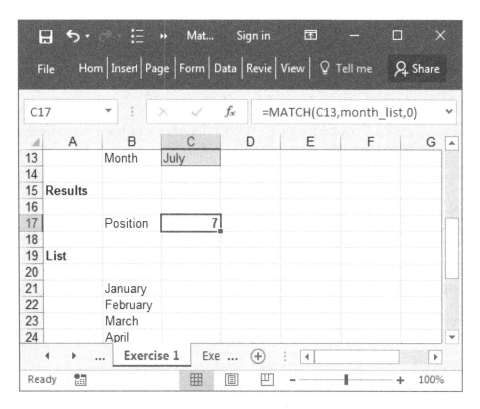

**Figure 19**

To prepare the worksheet for our MATCH function, we quickly assign the month list the name **month_list**. We use the Input cell style on the input cell, **C13**. We provide a drop-down by using data validation and allowing a list equal to **month_list**. Then we set up the following formula:

```
=MATCH(C13,month_list,0)
```

**Where:**

- **C13** is the value to look up, the month name input cell.

- **month_list** is where we are looking, in the month list.

- **0** tells Excel we are doing an exact match.

 **KB**

To write the formula with your keyboard, try these steps. To insert the function, =MA and then Tab to insert MATCH into the cell. To define the first argument, Ctrl+Up Arrow to jump up to **C13**, and Comma to begin the next argument. To define the second argument, Left Arrow, Ctrl+Down Arrow to get to the first list value, Ctrl+Shift+Down Arrow to select the list range, and Comma to start the next argument. To define the third argument, Down Arrow to select 0, Tab to insert. Type a closing parenthesis and hit Enter.

Now select different months and verify that the MATCH function returns the expected result. If not, ensure that the third argument of the MATCH function is set to 0.

At this point you should have a good idea that the function returns the relative position of an item in a list. Rarely, if ever, do I write a formula that uses the MATCH function only. I typically use the MATCH function as an argument for another function. Before we nest the MATCH function, let's take a moment to explore the VLOOKUP limitation mentioned above.

## EXERCISE 2—VLOOKUP LIMITATION

In this exercise we'll explore the limitation discussed and see it in action. We'll build a report using a VLOOKUP function, insert a new column into our worksheet, and then observe how the VLOOKUP function doesn't automatically update itself to keep up with this new column.

 **PRACTICE**

To work along, please refer to the Exercise 2 worksheet.

Our worksheet contains a departments table, which includes the department name, rollup group, manager, and employee count.

To prepare the worksheet, we name the department range *dept_lookup*. Next we populate the manager column of our report with a formula that retrieves the value from the department lookup range based on the department number stored in cell *B13*:

```
=VLOOKUP(B13,dept_lookup,4,0)
```

**Where:**

- **B13** is the value we are looking up, the department number.

- **dept_lookup** is the range in which we are looking, the department lookup range.

- **4** is the column that contains the value we want to return, the manager column.

- **0** means we are not performing a range lookup.

We fill the formula down, and everything works great.

Next month we open up the workbook and insert a new column into the worksheet somewhere between the first column and the manager column. The manager name moves from the fourth to the fifth column. The VLOOKUP no longer returns the manager, because the third argument is still a 4 instead of a 5. The VLOOKUP did not adjust for the inserted column.

Go ahead and verify this now. See how it breaks?

 **NOTE**

> The VLOOKUP formula will break only when the column is inserted between the first column and the column we are returning. It will not break when the new column is inserted outside of this range.

I wanted to be sure that you had a chance to see this VLOOKUP limitation occur in a real worksheet. Now let's improve VLOOKUP with MATCH.

## EXERCISE 3—VLOOKUP WITH MATCH

In this exercise, we'll nest a MATCH function in a VLOOKUP to work around the static third column limitation.

 **PRACTICE**

To work along, please refer to the Exercise 3 worksheet.

To prepare the worksheet, we name the department range *departments*. Next, to make it easy to refer to the header row of the department range, we name the header row *fields*, as shown in Figure 20 below.

 **NOTE**

Naming both ranges is not a requirement of performing this technique; it just makes life easier because we can use names instead of A1 style references in the functions.

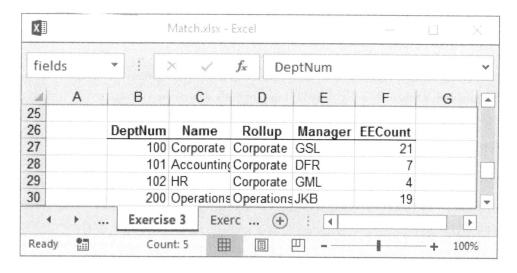

**Figure 20**

Now that the worksheet is prepared, let's write the lookup formula. Rather than try to write it all at once, let's write it in two steps. We'll start by getting the VLOOKUP working properly with an integer for the third argument. When the VLOOKUP is working, we will replace the integer with a MATCH function.

Since we want to retrieve the manager for the department number stored in *B16*, we use the following formula:

```
=VLOOKUP(B16,departments,4,0)
```

**Where:**

• **B16** is the value we are looking up, the department number.

- **departments** is the range in which we are looking, the department lookup range.

- **4** is the column number that has the value we want to return, the manager column.

- **0** means we are not performing a range lookup.

Fill the formula down, and verify that the expected results are returned. So far so good.

Now comes step 2, replacing the static integer 4 with a MATCH function. We will ask the MATCH function to figure out which column number contains the manager values. It will find the field label in the horizontal list of field headers (*fields*) and return the relative position. Currently, we expect the MATCH function to return 4, because the manager values are in the fourth column.

The following MATCH function should do the trick:

```
=MATCH(C$15,fields,0)
```

**Where:**

- **C$15** is the value we are trying to match, the cell that contains the column label. We use an absolute row reference so that as we fill the formula down, the reference stays locked onto the correct cell.

- **fields** is the range in which we are looking, the range of column labels.

- **0** tells Excel we are performing an exact match.

When we substitute the MATCH function for the static third argument in the VLOOKUP function, we get this beautiful formula:

```
=VLOOKUP(B16,departments,MATCH(C$15,fields,0),0)
```

**Where:**

- **B16** contains the value we are trying the find, the department number.

- **departments** is the range in which we are looking, the departments range.

- **MATCH(C$15,fields,0)** returns the relative column number of the value we wish to return.

- **Where:**

  - **C$15** is the value we are trying to find, the column label.

  - **fields** is the range in which we are looking, the row that contains the column headers.

  - **0** tells Excel to perform an exact match.

- **0** means we are not performing a range lookup.

Now, and this is the best part, insert a new column between **D** and **E**, and verify that this action did not break your formula as it did in the last exercise. Wow…pretty cool!

 **NOTE**

It's important that the second argument of the MATCH function begins in the same column as the second argument of the VLOOKUP function. Since the MATCH function returns the relative position number of the selected item, the position number needs to coincide with the VLOOKUP's range argument; otherwise, the wrong column will be returned.

## EXERCISE 4—TABLES

In this exercise, we'll use a VLOOKUP function to retrieve a value from a table.

 **PRACTICE**

To work along, please refer to the Exercise 4 worksheet.

In this worksheet, we have several columns that pull values from a table, as shown in Figure 21. One approach would be to write a unique VLOOKUP function for each column, where each function uses a different static integer value for the third argument to control which value to return. This means we could fill the formulas down, but not to the right.

As you know, whenever possible, it's preferred to write formulas that are consistent within a region.

 **XREF**

Writing formulas that are consistent within a region is discussed in Volume 1, Chapter 16.

Consistent formulas are easy to update because you can update the formula in the top left cell and then fill it down and right.

Rather than write a unique formula for each column, let's write a single formula that we can fill down and to the right. Using the MATCH function as the third VLOOKUP argument enables us to do this and to comply with the formula consistency principle. Let's do it.

In our last exercise, we prepared the worksheet by defining two named references, one for the department lookup range and one for the field headers. In practice I prefer to use tables, so in this exercise, we'll prepare our worksheet for our use by converting the department range into a table named *tbl_depts*.

Our worksheet has the department numbers, and we need to build the report formulas that populate the name, rollup, and manager columns by retrieving values from *tbl_depts*. We choose to do this with our new favorite pair of functions: VLOOKUP and MATCH.

Let's write the formula in two steps. Step one is to get the VLOOKUP function working with an integer value as the third argument. Step two is to substitute the MATCH function for the integer.

Here is the resulting formula, which we can fill down and right:

```
=VLOOKUP($B14,tbl_depts,MATCH(C$13,tbl_depts[#Headers],0),0)
```

**Where:**

- **$B14** is the value we are trying the find, the department number. Note the use of an absolute column reference so that as we fill right, the formulas continue to use the values in column **B**.

- **tbl_depts** is the range in which we are looking, the departments table.

- **MATCH(C$13,tbl_depts[#Headers],0)** returns the column number that has the value we want to return.

- **Where:**

  - **C$13** contains the value we are trying to match, the column label. Note the use of an absolute row reference, so that as we fill down the formulas continue to refer to the column labels stored in row *13*.

  - **tbl_depts[#Headers]** is the range in which we are trying to find the column label, in the headers row of the department table. Note the use of a structured table reference.

  - **0** tells the MATCH function we are performing an exact match.

- **0** tells the VLOOKUP function we are not performing a range lookup.

We fill the formula down and to the right, and the resulting report is shown in Figure 21 below.

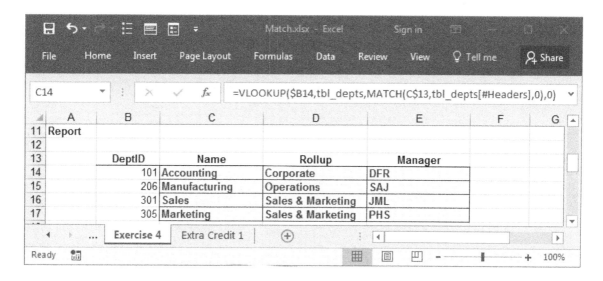

**Figure 21**

We've just accomplished a couple of different things. First, we used tables and structured table references. This is more efficient than setting up custom named references, and you can see how easy it was to refer to just the header row of the table, since there is a structured table reference designed for it. Next we used the VLOOKUP/MATCH combination, which is awesome because as new columns are inserted into the workbook, our formulas continue to work. Last we used consistent formulas in the report range, which makes them easy to update, since we can change the upper-left formula in the range and then fill it down and to the right, and it will continue to work. This is much better than having unique formulas for each column, which requires updating three formulas instead of one.

## CHAPTER CONCLUSION

Wow, that was so fun! Once you clearly understand this approach, you can use it often to enhance VLOOKUP functions, reduce errors, and improve productivity. For the most part, any VLOOKUP formulas used in recurring-use workbooks benefit from substituting the MATCH function for the third argument. That's what I call improving VLOOKUP with MATCH!

# Chapter 7: Improve VLOOKUP with VALUE and TEXT

## SET UP

One aspect of the VLOOKUP function that often yields confusing results is the fact that text values don't match numeric values. Let's take a moment to unpack this statement.

The VLOOKUP function doesn't match values when the cells are different data types. For example, the value of 100 can be entered into a cell and stored as either a number or as a text string. Typically, when a user types 100 into a cell, Excel interprets the entry and stores the value as a number. But depending on how the cell was formatted or if the value was imported, the value could be stored as a text string. You can get an indication of the data type by the default cell alignment. If the value is right-aligned then it is numeric; if it's left-aligned then it is text. The VLOOKUP function does not recognize a match between a value of 100 stored in one cell as a number and another cell as a text string.

Since VLOOKUP does not match equivalent values if stored as different data types, a common workaround is to convert text strings manually into numeric values and then perform the lookup. However, since that adds a manual step into a recurring process, and our goal is to remove manual steps from recurring processes, we'll take the time to figure out formulas that work with the data as it comes. Let's see how the TEXT and VALUE functions can help us write formulas that bypass this limitation of the VLOOKUP function.

# HOW TO

Rather than manually change the data type of the stored values, we'll use conversion functions in our formulas. They will not actually change the stored cell values. They will convert the values used in the evaluation of the formula and enable our lookup functions to work with the original stored values.

We need to know two worksheet functions to accomplish our objective: VALUE and TEXT.

The VALUE function returns a numeric value when given a text string that represents a number—that is, it converts a text string to a number. The syntax for this function follows:

=VALUE(text)

**Where:**

- **text** is a text string that represents a number.

The reciprocal to this function is the TEXT function, which returns a text string when given a numeric value—that is, it converts a number to a text string. The syntax for this function follows:

```
=TEXT(value, format_text)
```

**Where:**

- **value** is the value we wish to convert.

- **format_text** is the format we wish to apply to the text.

The format_text argument tells Excel exactly how to format the text string. The supported format codes are the same used to format any cell, such as "$#,###.00." You could use 0, without quotes, if you don't need a fancy format. You could use "General" or any of the other codes found in the Custom number format category in the Format Cells dialog box, including date format codes. For a complete list, reference the built-in Excel help system.

Now that we have covered the overview of these two functions, let's try our hand at some exercises.


# EXAMPLES

These hands-on exercises will help us practice using the TEXT and VALUE functions.

 **PRACTICE**

To work along, please refer to *Value Text.xlsx.*

**VIDEO**

To watch the solutions video, please visit the Excel University Video Library.

## EXAMPLE 1—THE PROBLEM

This example illustrates the problem we are trying to solve.

**PRACTICE**

To work along, please refer to the Exercise 1 worksheet.

We have a list of transactions and need Excel to look up each transaction's ZIP code from the ZIP code lookup range and return the corresponding city name. The transactions were exported from our accounting system into Excel, and some of the ZIPs are stored as number values and some are stored as text values. This is shown in column *E* in Figure 22 below.

The ZIP code lookup range is stored in a table named ***tbl_zips***.

Since the first ZIP code is stored in *E13*, we use the following formula:

```
=VLOOKUP(E13,tbl_zips,2,0)
```

**Where:**

- **E13** is the value we are trying to look up, the ZIP code.

- **tbl_zips** is the lookup range, the ZIP code table.

- **2** is the column that has the value we want to return, the city column.

- **0** tells Excel we are not performing a range lookup.

When we fill the formula down, we notice that it works for many ZIP codes, but not all. For some ZIP codes, the VLOOKUP returns the #N/A error code. We notice it returns this error for all ZIP codes stored as text values, which are those ZIPs that begin with a zero, as shown in Figure 22 below.

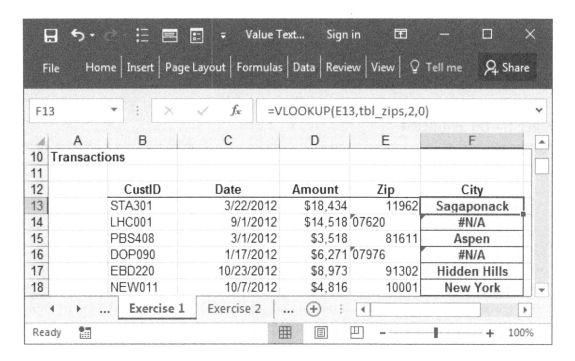

**Figure 22**

When presented with this type of situation, many Excel users manually convert the stored values so that both lists are of the same data type. For example, they convert the ZIP codes stored as text strings into numbers. Since this is a recurring-use workbook, and our goal is to eliminate manual steps from recurring processes, we'll take the time to write formulas that deal with the data as it comes to us. This brings us to our next exercise.

## EXAMPLE 2—VALUE

In this exercise, we'll use the VALUE function to resolve the errors encountered in the first exercise.

 **PRACTICE**

To work along, please refer to the Exercise 2 worksheet.

We'll use the same ZIP code table that we used in the previous exercise, named *tbl_zips*. If we take a look at it, we'll notice that all ZIP codes are stored as numeric values, and none are stored as text values. However, the transaction ZIP codes are mixed, and some are stored as text values while others as numbers.

We need a way to convert the transaction ZIP codes to numeric values so that they'll match the ZIP codes in *tbl_zips*. Fortunately, we know just such a conversion function: VALUE. Rather than look up the ZIP code found in the transactions range (cell *E13*), we'll use the VALUE function as the first argument to the VLOOKUP function so that it looks up the converted ZIP code:

```
=VLOOKUP(VALUE(E13),tbl_zips,2,0)
```

**Where:**

- **VALUE(E13)** converts the transaction ZIP code into a numeric value.

- **Where:**

    - **E13** is the value to convert, the transaction ZIP code.

- **tbl_zips** is the range in which we are looking, the ZIP code table.

- **2** is the column that has the value we wish to return, the city column.

- **0** tells Excel we are not performing a range lookup.

 **NOTE**

While you are getting warmed up, please note that it is just fine to write the formula in two steps rather than one. You can write the VLOOKUP function first and press Enter to store it in the cell. Then go back into the formula and substitute the VALUE function for the first VLOOKUP argument.

When we fill the formula down, it works, as shown in Figure 23 below.

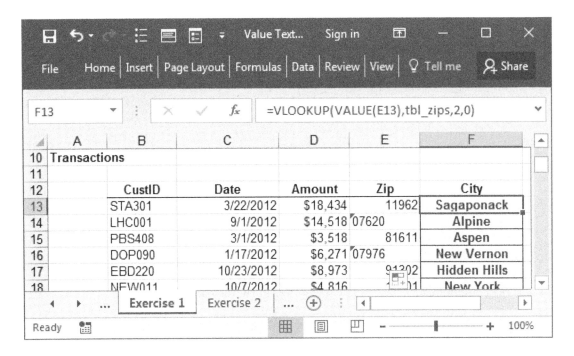

**Figure 23**

It works because Excel is not trying to look up the transaction ZIP codes—rather, it is looking up the converted ZIP codes. Since both the first and second function arguments of the VLOOKUP contain the same data type—numeric values—the VLOOKUP can make the match and return the expected result.

That is how you convert a value stored as a text string to a number. Now, what if you need to do the reverse and convert a number to a text string? The reciprocal function is TEXT. Let's check it out in the next exercise.

## EXAMPLE 3—TEXT

In this exercise, we'll use the TEXT function to convert a numeric value into a text value.

 **PRACTICE**

To work along, please refer to the Exercise 3 worksheet.

Here we have a vendor list that contains the vendor ID and the name. We also have a transaction list that contains the vendor ID, date, and amount. We need to retrieve the vendor name from the vendor list using a lookup function based on the ID.

The problem is that all the IDs in the vendor list are stored as text values, while the IDs in the transaction range are mixed. Specifically, when the vendor ID contains one or more letters, such as SMI333 or KEY201, Excel stores the ID as a text value. When the vendor ID does not contain letters, Excel stores it as a number, such as 40022 or 40012.

As you might suspect, when we use VLOOKUP alone, we receive #N/A errors. We decide to get help from the TEXT function.

We prepare the worksheet by first converting the vendor range into a table named *tbl_vendors*.

Since the first vendor ID is stored in *B12*, we use the following formula:

```
=VLOOKUP(TEXT(B12,0),tbl_vendors,2,0)
```

**Where:**

- **TEXT(B12,0)** is the value we are looking up, the value converted to a text.

- **Where:**

    - **B12** is the value to convert, the vendor ID.

    - **0** is the format code.

- **tbl_vendors** is the range in which we are looking, the vendor table.

- **2** is the column number that has the value we want to return, the vendor name column.

- **0** means we are not performing a range lookup.

We fill the formula down, and it works!

## EXAMPLE 4—MANUAL CONVERSION WITH PASTE SPECIAL

In this example, we'll explore my favorite way to manually convert numeric values stored as text to numbers.

 **PRACTICE**

To work along, please refer to the Exercise 4 worksheet.

If the worksheet is not used on a recurring basis, and we just want to manually convert numeric values stored as text into numbers, how can we do it? Well, this is Excel, so there are many ways, but I want to share with you my favorite way.

Before we cover the actual technique, let me start by asking a question: do you know what happens when you copy an empty cell? The answer is that you store a zero in the clipboard.

Have you ever explored the Paste Special dialog box? There are some incredible capabilities sitting in there, and I'd recommend you play with it and check out some of the cool stuff. For now, however, I'd like you to focus on the Operation section of the Paste Special dialog box, shown in Figure 24 below.

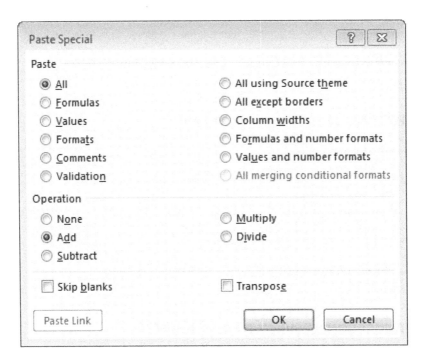

**Figure 24**

The Operation section includes some mathematical functions, such as Add and Multiply. When you select an Operation, Excel takes what is on the clipboard and applies the mathematical operation to all cells in the destination range. As an example, if we stored a zero on the clipboard and then used Paste

Special and selected the Add Operation, Excel would add 0 to all cells in the destination range. If the destination range contained numeric values stored as text strings, forcing the math on the cells will force Excel to change the data type of the stored value to a number.

Since this operation can be applied to an entire range of cells at once and since it is relatively easy to execute this entire process using the keyboard only, converting a range to numbers is fast.

Let's try it with our worksheet. We want to convert all values in the ZIP column to numbers. The steps are laid out sequentially below.

**Step 1: Place a zero on the clipboard.** You can place a zero on the clipboard by navigating to any empty cell and copying it.

 **KB**

> The keyboard command to copy is Ctrl+C.

**Step 2: Highlight the destination range.** Select the destination range for the upcoming Paste Special command, which in our case is the ZIP code column.

 **KB**

> Navigate to the first ZIP code in the column, and then extend the selection down to the end by pressing and holding the Ctrl and Shift keys, and then hitting the Down Arrow key.

**Step 3: Paste Special > Add.** Perform a Paste Special and use the Add Operation. This will add whatever is on the clipboard—in our case 0—to all cells in the destination range. Forcing Excel to perform this math will also force Excel to change the stored data type from text to number.

 **KB**

> The keyboard sequence is Alt+E, S, D, Enter (Edit, Paste Special, Add). Alternatively is Alt+H, V, S, D, Enter, which uses the Ribbon Tab accelerator keys.

Using this sequence is my preferred approach to performing this task, since I can keep my hands on the keyboard.

After we perform the conversion, all ZIP codes in the transactions list are stored as numbers. Since the lookup range *tbl_zips* is also stored as numbers, the VLOOKUP can perform its task just fine. We use this function:

```
=VLOOKUP(E14,tbl_zips,2,0)
```

**Where:**

- **E14** is the value we are trying to find, the ZIP code.

- **tbl_zips** is the range in which we are looking, the ZIP code table.

- **2** is the column number that has the value we want to return, the city column.

- **0** tells Excel we are not doing a range lookup.

We fill the formula down, and it works.

## CHAPTER CONCLUSION

In this chapter we addressed a common pitfall of the VLOOKUP function, which is the fact that the function does not match values if their data types are different. We addressed the issue by using nested conversion functions, VALUE and TEXT, as well as a manual method that uses the Paste Special > Add operation. I hope these approaches will help as you encounter related situations in your workbooks.

# Chapter 8: Moving Beyond VLOOKUP with INDEX

## SET UP

Another limitation of the VLOOKUP function is that it can't go left. Can't go left? Yes, it's a righty, can't go left. It can't return results that are to the left of the lookup column. This is because the lookup column must be the first column within the lookup range. It would perhaps be nice if we could specify a negative third argument, say -2, to go two columns to the left, but alas, that option does not exist to my knowledge. Thus, if the column we want to return the value from is to the left of the lookup column, we must physically move the return column to the right of the lookup column. But as you know, we strive to remove manual steps from recurring processes and prefer to take the time to figure out the formulas that will work with the data as it comes.

In this chapter we'll discuss the INDEX/MATCH combination, which doesn't suffer from this limitation. Please note that, unlike the previous two chapters, which demonstrated how to work around certain limitations by nesting additional functions into the VLOOKUP function, this chapter moves beyond VLOOKUP entirely.

While the VLOOKUP function is probably the most used, best known, and most popular lookup function, it probably shouldn't be, and once you discover the utility of the INDEX function, you may agree. The VLOOKUP function is the cornerstone of Excel's lookup functions, and, in my opinion, it should be thoroughly understood. Discovering the VLOOKUP function is sort of a rite of passage and an indicator of Excel proficiency. It is the function that forces a user to begin to see things differently and is one of the best ways to begin to understand lookup functions. For the record, I love the VLOOKUP function and can't even count the number of hours it has saved me over the years. But, even so, it is time to begin to move beyond VLOOKUP and to expand our toolset to include other lookup functions. Without further ado, I want to introduce the incredible INDEX function.

## HOW TO

The INDEX function returns a value from a range at a given position. Close your eyes and think about that for a moment.

*The INDEX function returns a value from a range at a given position.*

Can you see that yet?

The last time I asked you to close your eyes was in Chapter 6: Improve VLOOKUP with MATCH when we discussed the MATCH function. The MATCH function returns the relative position number of an item. The INDEX function actually returns the value in the cell, not the position number. Can you see how these two functions are similar, but the value that is returned is different? MATCH returns the position; INDEX returns the cell value.

This conceptual understanding is critical to working through the exercises. So, one more time: the INDEX function returns a value from a range at a given position. The MATCH function returns the position. We'll use these closely related lookup functions together in the formulas that follow.

Since we previously covered the arguments of the MATCH function, let's explore the INDEX function:

```
=INDEX(array, row_num,[column_num])
```

**Where:**

- **array** is the range that has the value you wish to return.

- **row_num** is the row number within the range that contains the value to return.

- **[column_num]** is the optional column number within the range that contains the value to return. This can be used to perform either one or two-dimensional lookups.

 **NOTE**

There are technically two forms of the INDEX function, referred to as the array form and the reference form. The scope of this book explores only the array form.

For more information about the reference form, please use the Excel help files.

You define a lookup range, called the array, in the first argument. Then you tell Excel how many rows down to go via the second argument. Then, optionally, you tell Excel to go a certain number of columns across via the third argument.

INDEX alone can't replace the VLOOKUP, but INDEX with MATCH can. Here's how: as we've established, the INDEX function returns a cell value from a range at a given position, specifically at a position specified by the row_num and, optionally, column_num arguments. The INDEX function expects you to enter a value for the row_num, such as 3 for the third row or 5 for the fifth row. However, we will use the MATCH function instead of an integer.

The main thing to keep in mind is this: in one-dimension lookups, the INDEX array is the single column that contains the value you want to return.

It will help to see this visually, and then we'll move to the exercises. In Figure 25 below, you'll notice that we want to allow a user to enter an account number into cell *C11*. We want a formula to retrieve the corresponding account name into cell *C12*.

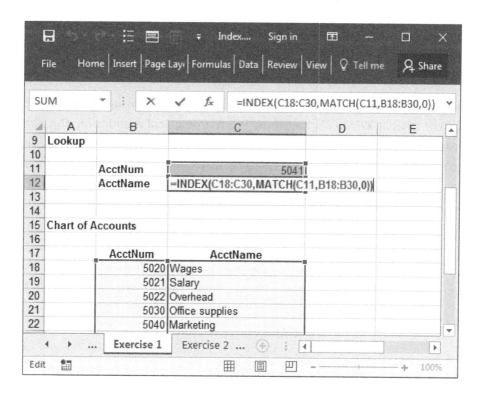

**Figure 25**

As you can see in the screenshot, we used the INDEX and MATCH functions in the formula. The INDEX function retrieves a value from the account name column, which is the range specified by the first argument *C18:C30*. The second argument tells Excel which row to retrieve. We use a MATCH function for the second argument to figure out which row has the value we want returned. The MATCH function finds the account number, cell *C11*, in the list of account numbers, *B18:B30*, and returns the position number to the INDEX function. This tells the INDEX function which row has the value to return. The optional third argument of the INDEX function is omitted for now to simplify the formula while we are getting warmed up.

 **NOTE**

The row_num argument is not the worksheet's absolute row number—rather, it is the relative row number within the array argument.

 **NOTE**

It is important to note that the range references in both the INDEX and MATCH functions need to start and end on the same row for the formula to return accurate results.

 **NOTE**

There are some interesting online discussions and performance tests that compare VLOOKUP to INDEX/MATCH methods. From a practical standpoint, the performance difference with smaller data sets doesn't seem significant enough to warrant one approach over the other, and since INDEX/MATCH is more flexible, it is my preferred approach. However, if you perform lookups on large data sets and performance is a concern, please feel free to explore the discussions online or test the two methods.

Let's do some hands-on work now.

# EXAMPLES

We'll explore several worksheets to get comfortable working with the INDEX and MATCH functions.

 **PRACTICE**

To work along, please refer to **Index.xlsx.**

 **VIDEO**

To watch the solutions video, please visit the Excel University Video Library.

## EXERCISE 1—ONE DIMENSION

In this exercise, we'll warm up with a simple, one-dimensional lookup.

 **PRACTICE**

To work along, please refer to the Exercise 1 worksheet.

To get started using this combinations of functions, we'll look up an account name. We want to allow the user to enter a valid account number into an input cell, and we want Excel to look up the account number in the chart of accounts and return the corresponding account name.

To prepare the worksheet, we highlight the input cell and apply data validation to it so that the user can select a valid account number from the chart of accounts.

Now it is time to write the formula so that when the user enters the account number in *C11*, Excel retrieves the related account name, as shown in Figure 26 below.

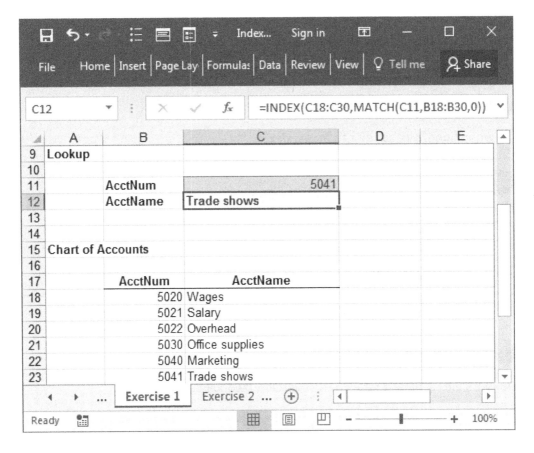

Figure 26

Here is the formula that performs the lookup:

```
=INDEX(C18:C30,MATCH(C11,B18:B30,0))
```

**Where:**

- **C18:C30** is the range that has the value we want to return, the account name column.

- **MATCH(C11,B18:B30,0)** tells the INDEX function which row to return.

- **Where:**

  - **C11** is the value to look up, the account number.

  - **B18:B30** is where to look, the account number column.

  - **0** tells Excel to perform an exact match.

At first you may think that you could more easily approach this exercise with a VLOOKUP, and you'd be right. This particular example can be accomplished with a single VLOOKUP rather than nesting INDEX and MATCH. But we are just getting warmed up, and soon we'll apply these functions to an exercise that could not be achieved with VLOOKUP.

## EXERCISE 2—WITH TABLES

In this exercise, we'll use INDEX/MATCH with a table.

 **PRACTICE**

To work along, please refer to the Exercise 2 worksheet.

We have a list of transactions, and this list contains the account number but not the account name. We need to retrieve the account name from the chart of accounts for all transactions.

To prepare the worksheet, we begin by converting the chart of accounts range into a table named *tbl_coa*.

We write the following lookup formula to retrieve the account name for the first account number in *E13*:

    =INDEX(tbl_coa[AcctName],MATCH(E13,tbl_coa[AcctNum],0))

Where:

- **tbl_coa[AcctName]** contains the value we want to return, the account name.

- **MATCH(E13,tbl_coa[AcctNum],0)** tells the INDEX function which row contains the value we want to return.

- **Where**

  - **E13** is the value we are trying to match, the account number.

  - **tbl_coa[AcctNum]** is where we are looking for the account number.

  - **0** tells Excel to perform an exact match.

We fill the formula down, and we've got it. Now let's see how INDEX/MATCH works around one of the key limitations of VLOOKUP, the ability to go left.

# EXERCISE 3—GOING LEFT

In this exercise, we'll practice going left with INDEX/MATCH.

 **PRACTICE**

To work along, please refer to the Exercise 3 worksheet.

We have a list of transactions that includes the item ID. We need to retrieve from the master items table other attributes about each item ID, such as the product manager and the product class.

Let's prepare the worksheet by converting the items range into a table named *tbl_items*.

Let's observe the items table, shown in Figure 27. We notice that the item ID column (ItemID) is in the middle of the table. Additionally, we observe that the values we want to return, the product manager (ProdMgr) and product class (Class), are to the left of the item ID lookup column.

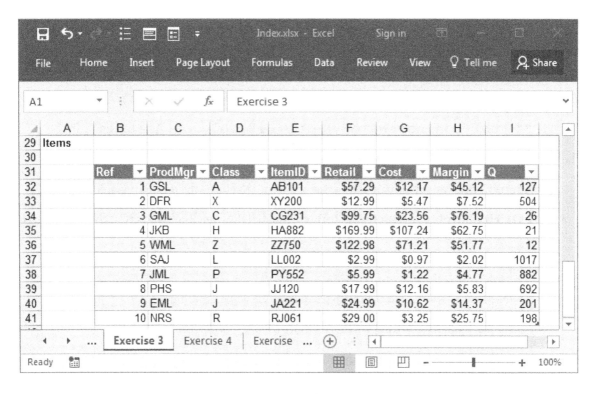

**Figure 27**

We need to look up the item ID and return a value that is to the left of it. This can't be accomplished with the VLOOKUP function. A common workaround is to cut and paste the lookup column so that it is the left-most column within the lookup range. If this were a one-time process, that approach might be just fine. However, in recurring processes we prefer to process the data as it comes. Otherwise we'll have to cut and paste each period, which is the type of manual step we want to eliminate from recurring processes. We'll take the time to set up a formula that deals with the data as it comes. In this case, it means using INDEX/MATCH instead of VLOOKUP.

Since the first item ID in our report is stored in cell *C13*, we write the following formula to retrieve the related product manager value from the table:

`=INDEX(tbl_items[ProdMgr],MATCH(C13,tbl_items[ItemID],0))`

**Where:**

- **tbl_items[ProdMgr]** is the column that has the value we want to return.

- **MATCH(C13,tbl_items[ItemID],0)** tells Excel which row has the value to return.

- **Where:**

    - **C13** is the value we are trying to match, the item ID value.

    - **tbl_items[ItemID]** is where we are looking, the item ID column.

    - **0** tells Excel to perform an exact match.

We fill the formula down, and we've got it. We write a similar function to populate the class column, and we are done.

In Excel University—Volume 1, we discussed operating on data as it comes, meaning when we import data into Excel, we should generally seek to build formulas that operate on the data in the format in which it is provided so we don't have to manually reformat it. The INDEX/MATCH approach is a specific example of this concept.

 **XREF**

Working with data as it comes is discussed in Volume 1, Chapter 16.

## EXERCISE 4—INSERT COLUMN

In this exercise we'll use the INDEX/MATCH functions to retrieve a value from a table. We'll then insert a column and observe that the INDEX/MATCH formula continues to work as expected.

 **PRACTICE**

To work along, please refer to the Exercise 4 worksheet.

Here we have a list of transactions that includes the item ID. We need to retrieve other attributes about each item, such as the product manager and the product class, from the master items table.

Let's prepare the worksheet for use by converting the items range into a table named *tbl_item_lookup*.

Next let's observe the worksheet for a moment. We notice that the item ID column is in the middle of the items table. Using the same techniques as the previous exercise, we populate the product manager and class columns with a formula that uses the INDEX and MATCH functions. For example, here is the formula we use to populate the product manager column:

```
=INDEX(tbl_item_lookup[ProdMgr],
    MATCH(B14,tbl_item_lookup[ItemID],0))
```

**Where:**

- **tbl_item_lookup[ProdMgr]** is the column that has the value we want to return.
- **MATCH(B14,tbl_item_lookup[ItemID],0))** determines which row has the value to return.
- **Where:**
    - **B14** is the value we are seeking, the item ID.
    - **tbl_item_lookup[ItemID]** is where we are looking.
    - **0** tells Excel to perform an exact match.

We use this formula to populate the class column:

```
=INDEX(tbl_item_lookup[Class],
    MATCH(B14,tbl_item_lookup[ItemID],0))
```

**Where:**

- **tbl_item_lookup[Class]** is the column that has the value we want to return.

- **MATCH(B14,tbl_item_lookup[ItemID],0))** identifies the row that has the value to return.

- **Where:**

  - **B14** is the value we are trying to match.

  - **tbl_item_lookup[ItemID]** is where we are looking.

  - **0** tells Excel to perform an exact match.

Now, this is the exciting part. Go ahead and insert a new column between columns *H* and *I*. You'll notice that your lookup formulas continue to work as expected! The column insert did not break the formulas.

This example is important for a couple of reasons. First, it demonstrates how INDEX/MATCH formulas remain intact when the user inserts columns. Since the first argument of the INDEX function is a range, Excel updates the reference. So no workaround is needed, as it is with the VLOOKUP function.

Additionally, this exercise exemplifies the concept we discussed in Volume 1, of building bulletproof workbooks by trying to anticipate how a user could unintentionally break the workbook. A user can insert a column anywhere without inadvertently breaking the formulas.

 **XREF**

> Trying to anticipate how a user can break a workbook and addressing the risk is discussed in Volume 1, Chapter 19.

The approach used in this worksheet does have a problem though. Do you know what it is? The problem is that we don't have formula consistency, because the two lookup formulas are unique. We wrote two unique formulas and filled each of them down. We did not write a single formula and then fill it down and to the right. The first formula retrieved the product manager value, and the second formula retrieved the class value. Let's address this issue and enable formula consistency by using a two-dimensional lookup with INDEX/MATCH.

## EXERCISE 5—TWO DIMENSIONS

In this exercise we'll write a single formula and fill it down and to the right, and it will continue to work.

 **PRACTICE**

To work along, please refer to the Exercise 5 worksheet.

Thus far we have used the INDEX function to perform a lookup that returns a value from a single column. We have told Excel the column from which to return the value, and we've used the MATCH function to find the proper row. We have thus far specified only two function arguments: the column from which to return the value and the MATCH function to determine the row. In this exercise, we are going to perform a two-dimensional lookup. This means we'll provide three arguments for the INDEX function: a multicolumn range, a MATCH function to determine the correct row, and another MATCH function to determine the correct column. This essentially returns the cell that is at the intersection of the determined row and column.

Consider Figure 28 below, which shows the departments table (***tbl_depts***).

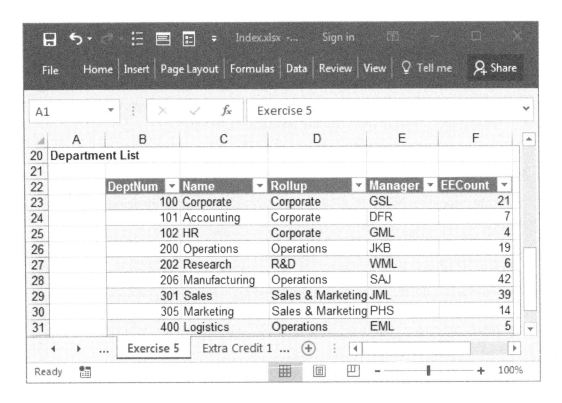

**Figure 28**

As you know, we can reference any cell in a worksheet by providing Excel with the column reference, such as *A*, and the row reference, such as *10*. The intersection is cell *A10*. Similarly, we can reference a value from the department table by the intersection of a table row and column. For example, the value SAJ lies at the intersection of the department 206 row and the manager column. This lookup logic is easily performed with the INDEX function. Recall that the function has the following syntax:

```
=INDEX(array, row_num,[column_num])
```

**Where:**

- **array** is the range that has the value you want to return.

- **row_num** is the row number within the range that contains the value to return.

- **[column_num]** is the optional column number within the range that contains the value to return.

We can specify a two-dimensional range, or a table, as the array argument. We can use a MATCH function for the row_num argument, and another MATCH function for the column_num argument.

Consider the report we are trying to build, in Figure 29 below.

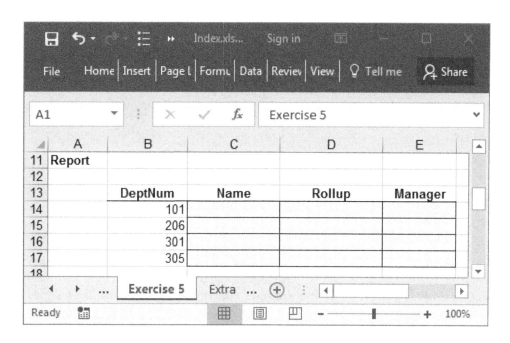

**Figure 29**

Our objective is to write a single formula in cell *C14* and then fill it down and to the right. This means that all formulas in the report range are consistent, and we like this very much. The INDEX function used in *C14* follows:

```
=INDEX(tbl_depts,
MATCH($B14,tbl_depts[DeptNum],0),
MATCH(C$13,tbl_depts[#Headers],0))
```

**Where:**

- **tbl_depts** is the range that contains the value we want to return.

- **MATCH($B14,tbl_depts[DeptNum],0)** tells the INDEX function which row to use.

- **Where:**

  - **$B14** is the value we are looking to match, our department number. Note the use of the absolute column reference so that as we fill the formula to the right the column that contains our department number (column *B*) continues to be used in the formula.

  - **tbl_depts[DeptNum]** is the range in which we are looking, the department number column.

  - **0** tells Excel to perform an exact match.

- **MATCH(C$13,tbl_depts[#Headers],0)** tells the INDEX function which column to use.

- **Where:**

  - **C$13** is the value we are looking to match, our column label. Note the use of an absolute row reference, so that as we fill the formula down the row that contains our column label (row *13*) continues to be used in the formula.

  - **tbl_depts[#Headers]** is the range in which we are looking, the headers row of the table.

  - **0** tells Excel to perform an exact match.

After writing the formula in *C14*, we fill it down and to the right and ensure that the formula provides the expected results. Which it does! Now we have a range with consistent formulas throughout, making the workbook easy to maintain over time. Nice work!

## CHAPTER CONCLUSION

The INDEX function is remarkable, and we've only just begun to explore it. We'll continue to use and refine this function as we proceed throughout the series.

# Chapter 9: Trap Errors with IFERROR

## SET UP

When using formula-based reports, especially when lookup functions are involved, we need to control the formula's result when it encounters an error. I'll refer to this effort as error trapping.

Excel errors such as the #N/A error can cause issues downstream. For example, any SUM function that has a sum range that includes a cell with #N/A will itself return #N/A. Sometimes this is exactly the behavior we want so we can adequately address any issues, but often, this creates problems.

Often we prefer to substitute a specific value for an error code, such as replacing #N/A with a 0. The idea of substituting a selected value in place of an error code is quite handy.

In the old days—prior to Excel 2007—substituting a desired value for an error was cumbersome and required nested functions. However, beginning with Excel 2007, Microsoft introduced the IFERROR function, which makes it super easy. Let's see how it works.

## HOW TO

The IFERROR function has two arguments, as follows:

```
=IFERROR(value, value_if_error)
```

**Where:**

- **value** is the value, cell reference, function, or formula to evaluate.

- **value_if_error** value to return if the value argument is any Excel error, such as #N/A or #DIV/0!.

Here is a simple example. If cell **A1** contains a value of 10, and cell **A2** contains a value of 0, then the formula =A1/A2 returns the #DIV/0! error. If we want Excel to return a 0 rather than #DIV/0!, then we simply wrap the IFERROR function around our formula, as follows:

```
=IFERROR(A1/A2,0)
```

**Where:**

- **A1/A2** is the value argument, which Excel will try to evaluate and return.

- **0** is the value to return if the first argument evaluates to any Excel error, such as #DIV/0!.

In this example, we told the formula to return 0 if A1/A2 evaluated to an error. We could have just as easily replaced the error with any other value or function, such as a dash, "-", or a label, "NA." Remember that text arguments need to be enclosed between quotation marks.

## EXAMPLES

Let's get some hands-on experience with the IFERROR function.

 **PRACTICE**

To work along, please refer to **Iferror.xlsx.**

 **VIDEO**

To watch the solutions video, please visit the Excel University Video Library.

## EXERCISE 1—VARIANCE

In this exercise, we'll compute the variance to budget and use the IFERROR function to ensure a clean report.

 **PRACTICE**

To work along, please refer to the Exercise 1 worksheet.

The actual SG&A results for last month are now available, and we need to compare them to the budget. We set up a worksheet that has the following columns: account, actual, budget, variance amount, and variance percent. The variance column is designed to show a positive value if the variance is favorable and a negative value if the variance is unfavorable. We are comparing expense values, and if actual is less than budget, we reflect a favorable variance. The variance percent column shows the variance amount divided by the budget amount.

In some cases, accounts with actual amounts have zero budget. For the rows without a budget amount, the variance percent formula returns a #DIV/0! error, such as row *14* in Figure 30 below.

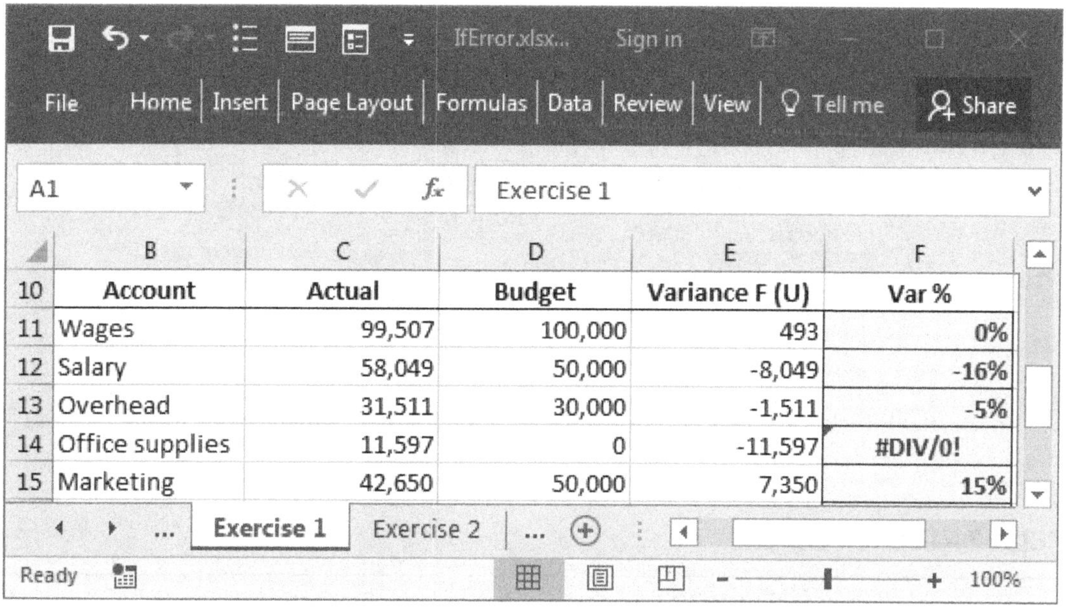

| | B | C | D | E | F |
|---|---|---|---|---|---|
| 10 | Account | Actual | Budget | Variance F (U) | Var % |
| 11 | Wages | 99,507 | 100,000 | 493 | 0% |
| 12 | Salary | 58,049 | 50,000 | -8,049 | -16% |
| 13 | Overhead | 31,511 | 30,000 | -1,511 | -5% |
| 14 | Office supplies | 11,597 | 0 | -11,597 | #DIV/0! |
| 15 | Marketing | 42,650 | 50,000 | 7,350 | 15% |



**Figure 30**

We want to clean up the report by replacing #DIV/0! errors with something else. Thus we use the following formula:

```
=IFERROR(E11/D11,"-")
```

**Where:**

- **E11/D11** computes the variance percent, and will be returned unless it is an error.
- **"-"** is the value to return in the event of an error.

The results are shown in Figure 31 below.

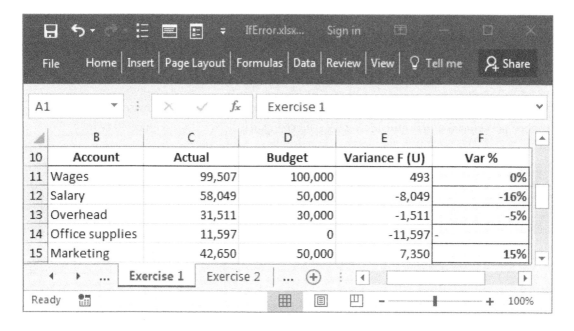

**Figure 31**

As you can see, the IFERROR function replaced the #DIV/0! error with a dash, which is perfect.

## EXERCISE 2—LOOKUP ERRORS

In this exercise, we'll use the IFERROR function to clean up a report that uses lookup functions.

 **PRACTICE**

> To work along, please refer to the Exercise 2 worksheet.

Let's assume that we need to export a monthly account activity report from our accounting system. While some accounting systems export all accounts and report zero for accounts with no monthly activity, our system excludes accounts without activity. We store this exported current month data in a table named *tbl_cm*.

We have created a formula-based report that lists all accounts and uses lookup formulas to retrieve the values from *tbl_cm*. When we use either the VLOOKUP or INDEX/MATCH functions with exact match logic, #N/A is returned when a matching account value is not found. For example, if we ask Excel to look up the account "Marketing" from a range that does not include "Marketing," Excel returns #N/A.

 **NOTE**

As discussed previously, exact-match logic is controlled by the fourth argument of the VLOOKUP function and the third argument of the MATCH function.

The key concept is this: when a lookup function uses exact match logic, it returns #N/A when the item being sought is not found. Understanding the concept enables us to do some cool things—for example, perform list comparisons. More on that later. For now, let's see how we can address this with error trapping.

 **XREF**

List comparisons are discussed in Chapter 11: List Comparisons.

As illustrated in row *17* in Figure 32 below, Excel returns #N/A when the lookup formula can't find a matching account value.

| | A | B | C | D |
|---|---|---|---|---|
| 12 | | **Account** | **Amount** | |
| 13 | | Wages | $99,507 | |
| 14 | | Salary | $58,049 | |
| 15 | | Overhead | $31,511 | |
| 16 | | Office supplies | $11,597 | |
| 17 | | Marketing | #N/A | |

Figure 32

We can easily trap this error by wrapping the IFERROR function around our lookup function, as follows:

```
=IFERROR(VLOOKUP(B13,tbl_cm,2,0),0)
```

**Where:**

- **VLOOKUP(B13,tbl_cm,2,0)** is the first argument and will be returned unless it evaluates to an error.

- **Where:**

    - **B13** is the value we are trying to find, the account.

    - **tbl_cm** is where we are looking.

    - **2** is the column that has the value we want to return, the amount.

    - **0** tells Excel we are not performing a range lookup and that we are using the exact match logic instead.

- **0** is the value to return if the first argument evaluates to an error.

When the formula is filled down, we see that 0 appears rather than #N/A, and that is exactly what we were hoping for. Nice!


## EXERCISE 3—DEPARTMENT ANALYSIS

In this exercise we'll replace an error generated by comparing the current month to the prior month SG&A expenses.

 **PRACTICE**

To work along, please refer to the Exercise 3 worksheet.

This worksheet compares current month to prior month SG&A expenses for each account. We include a column that computes the increase/decrease and a column that computes the percent increase/decrease. The percent increase/decrease is computed by dividing the increase/decrease by the prior month amount. When the prior month amount is zero, Excel returns the #DIV/0! error. We can easily substitute a 0 for the error by using the following formula:

```
=IFERROR(E11/D11,0)
```

**Where:**

- **E11/D11** divides the increase/decrease by the prior month amount.

- **0** is the value the function should return in the event that the first argument is an error.

Once this formula is filled down through the range, our report is complete.

## CHAPTER CONCLUSION

Having the ability to trap formula errors and return a substituted value is quite handy, and the IFERROR function is a perfect way to accomplish this task. I use it all the time and hope it is useful for you as well.

# Chapter 10: The IF Function

## SET UP

For a balance sheet to be accurate, assets must equal liabilities plus equity. Said another way, if assets equal liabilities plus equity, then the balance sheet is in balance; otherwise, the balance sheet contains an error. Think about that idea for a moment:

> *If* assets equal liabilities plus equity, *then* you are in balance; *otherwise*, you have an error.

The statement contains three parts. It has a condition to test—namely, do assets equal liabilities plus equity? It has a result when the test is true: the balance sheet is in balance. It has a different result when the test is not true: the balance sheet contains an error.

Excel's IF function is designed with identical logic and the same three parts. The IF function allows Excel to perform conditional computations and also to return a value based on the test results.

Having this ability within Excel is practical and useful, and it is for this reason that the IF function remains one of my favorites.

## HOW TO

The IF function evaluates a condition and then returns a value based on the results of the condition. There are three distinct pieces of information that the function needs to return its result: the condition to test, the value to return if the condition is true, and the value to return if the condition is false. The IF function thus has the following arguments:

```
=IF(logical_test,[value_if_true],[value_if_false])
```

**Where:**

- **logical_test** is the condition to test.
- **[value_if_true]** is the value to return if logical_test is TRUE.
- **[value_if_false]** is the value to return if logical_test is FALSE.

The logical test can be expressed as any value, comparison, or function that returns a TRUE or FALSE value. Each of the final two arguments, the values to return, can be expressed as a value, a function, or even another IF function.

## EXAMPLES

Let's get some hands-on practice.

 **PRACTICE**

To work along, please refer to *If.xlsx.*

 **VIDEO**

To watch the solutions video, please visit the Excel University Video Library.

## EXERCISE 1—BALANCE SHEET

In this exercise we'll use the IF function to determine if a balance sheet is in balance.

 **PRACTICE**

To work along, please refer to the Exercise 1 worksheet.

We prepare a balance sheet each month in Excel. We know that assets must equal liabilities plus equity, so we want Excel to test this condition. We decide to write an IF function that returns "Yes" when the balance sheet is in balance and "No" when it is not.

In the balance sheet, the total assets value resides in cell *C17*. Total liabilities plus equity is found in cell *C32*. This is the appropriate IF function:

```
=IF(C17=C32,"Yes","No")
```

**Where:**

- **C17=C32** is the condition to test, and returns TRUE when the balance sheet is in balance.

- **"Yes"** the value to return if the balance sheet is in balance.

- **"No"** the value to return if not.

Test the formula by changing the balance sheet values to ensure that the expected result is returned.

## EXERCISE 2—INCOME STATEMENT

In this exercise, we'll use the IF function to properly label an income statement.

 **PRACTICE**

To work along, please refer to the Exercise 2 worksheet.

We prepare an income statement each month. When there is a monthly net income, we like to label the net income line "Net Income." When there is a monthly loss, we prefer the label "Net Loss."

Since the income value is stored in *C24*, we use the following IF function:

```
=IF(C24>=0,"Net Income","Net Loss")
```

**Where:**

- **C24>=0** returns TRUE when *C24* is greater than or equal to 0.

- **"Net Income"** is the value to return when the first argument is TRUE.

- **"Net Loss"** is the value to return when the first argument is FALSE.

Test the formula to verify that it returns the expected result.

## EXERCISE 3—COMMISSION

In this exercise, we'll use an IF function to compute a commission amount.

 **PRACTICE**

To work along, please refer to the Exercise 3 worksheet.

Each month, we prepare the commission calculations. Our company's plan provides for a commission only when a rep sells more than the quota. If this is so, then the commission rate is applied to the excess. If not, then zero commission is reported.

The commission rate cell is named *rate*. We use the following IF function to compute the commission for the first rep, whose excess of sales over quote is stored in cell *E16*:

```
=IF(E16>0,E16*rate,0)
```

**Where:**

- **E16>0** returns TRUE if the excess of sales over quota is greater than zero.

- **E16*rate** applies the commission rate to the excess.

- **0** returns zero commission when sales are less than quota.

We fill the formula down and submit our commission worksheet to payroll!

## CHAPTER CONCLUSION

You can use the IF function in a wide variety of ways. I'm sure it is, or will soon be, one of your most frequently used functions.

# Chapter 11: List Comparisons

## SET UP

It is often convenient to compare two lists. A list comparison occurs when we have two separate ranges and want to identify which values in one appear on the other. For example, we have a check register and a list of checks that cleared the bank. We want Excel to tell us which checks on the check register cleared the bank. We can easily compare these lists with a lookup function.

## HOW TO

To perform a list comparison, we use the built-in behavior of Excel's lookup functions. Do you recall that the lookup functions VLOOKUP and MATCH both include the concept of an exact match? When we ask either lookup function to use exact match logic, the function returns an error code if the value being sought is not found in the related lookup range. We can use this behavior to perform list comparisons so that when a value is not found, an error code appears.

 **XREF**

VLOOKUP is discussed in Chapter 5: Lookup Basics.

 **XREF**

MATCH is discussed in Chapter 6: Improve VLOOKUP with MATCH.

If you prefer the VLOOKUP function, then you tell it to perform exact match logic by setting the fourth argument to FALSE, or 0. If you prefer the MATCH function, then you tell it to perform exact match logic by setting the third argument to 0.

## EXAMPLES

Let's practice with some hands-on exercises.

 **PRACTICE**

To work along, please refer to *List Comparisons.xlsx*.

 **VIDEO**

To watch the solutions video, please visit the Excel University Video Library.

### EXERCISE 1—MATCH

In this exercise, we'll use the MATCH lookup function to determine if a check cleared the bank.

 **PRACTICE**

To work along, please refer to the Exercise 1 worksheet.

The two ranges on the exercise worksheet represent the check register and the bank download. The check register was exported from the accounting system. The bank download was downloaded from our bank's website and represents the checks that have cleared the bank.

Our objective is to determine which checks on the register appear on the bank download. One option is to use the MATCH function. If you recall, the MATCH function returns the relative position number of a list item, and when the third argument is set to 0, returns an error code if the value is not found. When we use this function, our column will include an error code for all checks that do not appear on the bank download and the position for the checks that do.

We use the following formula:

```
=MATCH(B11,$B$28:$B$34,0)
```

**Where:**

- **B11** is the value we are looking for, the check number.

- **$B$28:$B$34** is where we are looking, on the bank download check column.

- **0** tells Excel to perform exact match logic.

**KB**

To write this formula with your keyboard, try these steps. To insert the function, =MA and Tab. To define the first argument, Left Arrow over to select **B11**, and then Comma to start the next argument. Ctrl+Left Arrow twice to jump to the first column, Ctrl+Down Arrow to jump to the end of the check register, Ctrl+Down Arrow to jump to the bank download, Down Arrow to select the first check number, Ctrl+Shift+Down Arrow to select the check column, F4 to lock the range reference, and Comma to begin the next argument. To define the third argument, Down Arrow to select 0, and Tab to insert. Close the parentheses and hit Enter.

When this formula is filled down, Excel returns an integer value when the check appears in the bank download and the #N/A error when the check does not appear. This outcome makes it fast and easy to see which checks haven't yet cleared the bank.

However, we prefer to return the amount of the check rather than its relative position. Let's try the VLOOKUP function next.

## EXERCISE 2—VLOOKUP

In this exercise, we'll use the VLOOKUP function to determine if a check cleared the bank.

**PRACTICE**

To work along, please refer to the Exercise 2 worksheet.

We want to know which checks cleared the bank. This time, however, we want to return the amount of the check rather than the check's position in the list. The following formula is perfectly suited for this task:

```
=VLOOKUP(B11,$B$28:$D$34,3,0)
```

**Where:**

- **B11** is the value we are seeking, the check number.

- **$B$28:$D$34** is the lookup range, the bank download range.

- **3** is the column number that contains the value we want to return, the amount.

- **0** tells Excel to use the exact match logic (we are not doing a range lookup).

When we fill the formula down, it's easy to identify which checks did not clear the bank, because they contain the #N/A error. For checks that did clear the bank, the formula retrieves the amount per the bank.

While this approach makes it easy to identify the individual checks that have not yet cleared the bank—those that have the #N/A error—we are unable to compute a total, since any error cells in the range cause a sum function to return an error as well. Can you think of a way to trap any errors? Did you say IFERROR? Great!

## EXERCISE 3—IFERROR

In this exercise, we'll use an IFERROR function to clean up the results.

 **PRACTICE**

To work along, please refer to the Exercise 3 worksheet.

We want to know which checks cleared the bank. For checks that haven't cleared, we prefer the formula return the phrase "Not Found" rather than #N/A.

To return the dollar amount for cleared checks and "Not Found" for others, we wrap the IFERROR function around the VLOOKUP function as follows:

```
=IFERROR(VLOOKUP(B11,$B$28:$D$34,3,0),"Not Found")
```

**Where:**

- **VLOOKUP(B11,$B$28:$D$34,3,0)** is the first argument of the IFERROR function. It returns the amount of the check if found and #N/A if not.

- **Where:**

  - **B11** is the value we are seeking, the check number.

- **$B$28:$D$34** is where we are looking, the bank download range.

- **3** is the column that has the value we want to return, the amount column.

- **0** tells Excel to use exact match logic.

- **"Not Found"** is the second argument of the IFERROR function.

We fill the formula down and notice a nice, clean bank reconciliation. In addition, the total works, since there are no #N/A errors in the sum range. Sweet!

## CHAPTER CONCLUSION

Surprisingly, the need to perform list comparisons is common, and the ability to quickly determine what items from one list appear on another list is useful. This is yet another practical application of the amazing Excel lookup functions.

# Chapter 12: The ISERROR Function

## SET UP

Thus far, we have explored one way to trap errors, which was the IFERROR function. There are other functions we can use for error trapping. This chapter explores the ISERROR function.

 **XREF**

The IFERROR function is discussed in Chapter 9: Trap Errors with IFERROR.

A couple of situations require the use of ISERROR rather than IFERROR. The first situation occurs in Excel versions earlier than 2007. The IFERROR function was introduced with Excel 2007 and is, therefore, unavailable in earlier versions. The second situation is when we want to perform a test and then return a different result than the test result when no error is found. Let's unpack that statement.

With the IFERROR function, you tell Excel to evaluate the first argument. If it is not an error, its value is returned. If it is an error, the second argument is returned. But what if you want to return a value other than the first argument when it is not an error? We'll need to use ISERROR instead.

As an example, let's assume we want to find out if a check number that appears on our check register also appears on the bank download. We want Excel to return "Cleared" if the check appears and "Outstanding" if it does not appear. Since this type of logic is unavailable with the IFERROR function, we'll use the ISERROR function.

# HOW TO

This is the syntax of the ISERROR function:

```
=ISERROR(value)
```

**Where:**

- **value** is the value to evaluate. Please note that this can be a value, cell reference, or function.

If the value argument is an error, the function returns TRUE; otherwise, it returns FALSE.

I rarely use this function on its own; I mostly use it as an argument to another function. For example, I'll use it as the first argument of an IF function. Consider the need to see if a check number on the check register appears on the bank download. If it does, we want to return "Cleared"; otherwise, we want to return "Outstanding." This is easily accomplished with a nested IF/ISERROR formula. Here is an example, with the VLOOKUP arguments removed for simplicity:

```
=IF(ISERROR(VLOOKUP()), "Outstanding", "Cleared")
```

**Where:**

- **ISERROR(VLOOKUP())** is the first argument of the IF function, the condition to test. ISERROR will return TRUE if the VLOOKUP value returns an error. ISERROR will return FALSE if the VLOOKUP does not return an error.

- **Where:**

  - **VLOOKUP()** looks for the check number from the register on the bank download. It will return a value if it is found. If it is not found, VLOOKUP returns an error code. This result is passed into the ISERROR function.

- **"Outstanding"** is returned by the IF function if ISERROR returns TRUE. ISERROR returns TRUE if the VLOOKUP returns an error, meaning that the check is not found on the bank download.

- **"Cleared"** is returned by the IF function if ISERROR returns FALSE. ISERROR returns FALSE if the VLOOKUP function returns a value rather than an error, meaning that the check is found on the bank download.

In this scenario, you could have just as easily used a MATCH function rather than a VLOOKUP function. MATCH returns an error if it can't find the check, and the IF function returns "Outstanding." If MATCH finds a check, the IF function returns "Cleared." So it really doesn't matter which lookup function you use, provided it returns an error when an item is not found.

I don't know about you, but I think it's time to jump into Excel to get a better feel for this.

## EXAMPLES

Let's get some practice.

 **PRACTICE**

To work along, please refer to *Iserror.xlsx.*

 **VIDEO**

To watch the solutions video, please visit the Excel University Video Library.

### EXERCISE 1—RECONCILIATION WITH MATCH

In this exercise, we'll perform a bank reconciliation using the MATCH function.

 **PRACTICE**

To work along, please refer to the Exercise 1 worksheet.

The first check in the check register is stored in cell **B13**. The bank download is stored in the range **B30:B36**. Following is the formula that returns "Cleared" if the check number is found in the bank download and "Outstanding" if not:

```
=IF(ISERROR(MATCH(B13,$B$30:$B$36,0)), "Outstanding",
"Cleared")
```

**Where:**

- **ISERROR(MATCH(B13,$B$30:$B$36,0))** is the first argument of the IF function, the condition to test.
- **Where:**

- **MATCH(B13,$B$30:$B$36,0)** is the argument of the ISERROR function, and returns an error if the check is not found in the bank download list.

- **Where:**

  - **B13** is the check number we are trying to find, the check number on the check register.

  - **$B$30:$B$36** is where we are looking, in the bank download. Note the use of absolute references so that this formula can be filled down and continue to refer to the correct bank download list.

  - **0** tells Excel to perform exact match logic—meaning, return an error if the check number is not found.

- **"Outstanding"** is returned by the IF function if the first argument is TRUE. If the check on the check register is not found on the bank download, then the ISERROR function returns TRUE.

- **"Cleared"** is returned by the IF function if the first argument is FALSE. If the check on the check register is found on the bank download, then the ISERROR function returns FALSE.

After writing this formula for the first check in the check register, we fill it down and instantly see which checks have cleared the bank and which have not.

## EXERCISE 2—RECONCILIATION WITH VLOOKUP

In this exercise, we'll perform a bank reconciliation using the VLOOKUP function.

 **PRACTICE**

To work along, please refer to the Exercise 2 worksheet.

We can use the VLOOKUP to perform list comparisons. When the fourth argument is FALSE, the function returns an error when the lookup value is not found. Let's use it inside an IF/ISERROR formula, similar to our previous exercise.

Assuming that the first check register number is stored in *B13*, and the bank download is stored in a table named ***bank_list***, then this is the appropriate formula:

```
=IF(ISERROR(VLOOKUP(B13,bank_list,1,0)),"Outstanding","Clea
red")
```

**Where:**

- **ISERROR(VLOOKUP(B13,bank_list,1,0))** is the first argument of the IF function and returns TRUE if the check is not found.

- **Where:**

  - **VLOOKUP(B13,bank_list,1,0)** is the argument of the ISERROR function and returns an error if the check is not found.

  - **Where:**

    - **B13** is the lookup value, the check number.

    - **bank_list** is the lookup range, the bank download.

    - **1** is the column that has the value we want to return. Note that it really doesn't matter which column we return, since it is not ultimately returned by the formula to the cell.

    - **0** tells Excel to use exact match logic and to return an error code if the lookup value is not found in the lookup range—that is, if the check number is not found in the bank download.

- **"Outstanding"** is returned by the IF function if the check is not found.

- **"Cleared"** is returned by the IF function if the check is found.

I know there are many moving parts to this formula, but this approach can be used in many different situations, especially in list comparisons.

## CHAPTER CONCLUSION

Well, that is a demonstration of the powerful combination of IF/ISERROR, and it has been used in countless workbooks. I hope it is useful in the work you are doing as well.

# Chapter 13: Multicolumn List Comparisons with COUNTIFS

## SET UP

Have you ever performed multicolumn list comparisons? If so, how have you approached this task? Have you combined the various columns into a single column using concatenation and then compared the single, combined column? If so I'd like to introduce you to an alternative way that eliminates the need to combine columns.

Let's discuss this a bit. Often we use a lookup formula to retrieve a related value from a list. Sometimes we use lookup formulas to perform list comparisons when we don't need to return a corresponding value but want to know if the value appears. For example, we want to know if an employee from one list appears in another list or if a check number appears on the check list.

When we need to compare only a single column—for example the check number—VLOOKUP and MATCH are just fine. If we need to compare multiple columns—for example, the first and last name columns—then these functions don't work as well, because to use them we would need to first combine multiple columns into a single lookup column. Combining two or more columns into a single lookup column is often achieved with concatenation.

 **XREF**

Concatenation is discussed in Chapter 19: Concatenation Basics.

Since our goal is to eliminate manual steps, we strive to work with the data as it comes to us. The step of combining multiple columns into a single lookup column is unnecessary when we use the COUNTIFS function to perform multicolumn list comparisons.

The COUNTIFS function is a conditional counting function that returns the count of cells that meet the specified condition or conditions. We can easily apply this function to multicolumn list comparisons. Let's explore the details.

 **NOTE**

> If instead of just knowing if a record appears in another list, you want to retrieve a numeric value, then you can use SUMIFS instead of COUNTIFS.

## HOW TO

COUNTIFS is a conditional counting function introduced with Excel 2007. The syntax resembles the SUMIFS function in that the criteria arguments are provided in pairs, as follows:

```
=COUNTIFS(criteria_range1, criteria1, …)
```

**Where:**

- **criteria_range1** is the range that has the cells to inspect and count.

- **criteria1** is the criteria value.

- **…** additional argument pairs.

Please note you can provide up to 127 range/criteria pairs. All ranges must be the same size, and wildcard characters are supported.

When using this function to perform multicolumn list comparisons, we essentially count the number of rows that meet all conditions. If the result is zero, we know the item does not appear on the list.

## EXAMPLES

Let's get some hands on use with several exercises.

 **PRACTICE**

To work along, please refer to *Multicolumn.xlsx.*

 **VIDEO**

To watch the solutions video, please visit the Excel University Video Library.

## EXERCISE 1—EMPLOYEES

In this exercise, we'll use the COUNTIFS function to compare multiple columns stored in two lists of employee records.

 **PRACTICE**

To work along, please refer to the Exercise 1 worksheet.

Our worksheet contains two employee lists. The first list contains the current employees, and the second list was generated last month. We want to identify new employees by determining which employees appear on the current list but not the prior-month list. Unfortunately, the data does not contain a unique identifier column, such as employee ID. If it did, we could easily use VLOOKUP or MATCH. Since we need to use both the first and last name columns to perform our comparison, we'll use the COUNTIFS function.

The prior-month list is stored in a table named *tbl_prior.* The first name of the first employee in the current-month is stored in *B13* and the last name is stored in *D13*. We write the following formula to determine if this employee appears in the prior-month list:

```
=COUNTIFS(tbl_prior[FirstName],B13,tbl_prior[LastName],D13)
```

**Where:**

- **tbl_prior[FirstName]** is the first criteria range, the first name column of the prior month list.

- **B13** is the first name in the current month list.

- **tbl_prior[LastName]** is the second criteria range, the last name column of the prior month list.

- **D13** is the last name in the current month list.

Since the COUNTIFS function counts the number of rows where all conditions are met, both the first and last name fields must match to be included in the result.

When the formula is filled down, we can easily see which employees do not appear on the prior-month list, since the COUNTIFS function returns a zero value for them.

## EXERCISE 2—EMPLOYEES WITH IF

In this exercise, we'll nest the COUNTIFS function inside an IF function to clean up the report.

 **PRACTICE**

To work along, please refer to the Exercise 2 worksheet.

The situation is the same as the previous exercise, except this time we want to clean up the output. Instead of having the formula return the count, we want the formula to return "New" when an employee is deemed new and "Existing" if the employee appears on the prior-month list.

This can be performed by wrapping an IF function around our previous function.

The following formula works perfectly:

```
=IF(COUNTIFS(tbl_prior[FirstName],B13,tbl_prior[LastName],D13)=0,"New","Existing")
```

**Where:**

- **COUNTIFS(tbl_prior[FirstName],B13,tbl_prior[LastName],D13)=0** is the first argument of the IF function and will return TRUE if the COUNTIFS function evaluates to zero—that is, when an employee is not found on the prior month list.

- **Where:**

    - **tbl_prior[FirstName]** is the range to inspect, the first name column of the prior month list.

    - **B13** is the employee first name.

    - **tbl_prior[LastName]** is the range to inspect, the last name column of the prior month list.

    - **D13** is the employee last name.

- **"New"** is the second argument of the IF function, and will be returned if the first argument is TRUE—that is, if the COUNTIFS function is equal to zero.

- **"Existing"** is the third argument of the IF function, and will be returned if the first argument is FALSE—that is, if the COUNTIFS function is not equal to zero.

Once the formula is filled down, it is easy to see which employees don't appear on the prior-month list, since they are marked as New.

## EXERCISE 3—ITEM RECONCILIATION

In this exercise, we'll reconcile the exports from two different systems.

 **PRACTICE**

**To work along, please refer to the Exercise 3 worksheet.**

Our company stores product data in two places: our online store and our accounting system. We want to identify those items that appear in our accounting system but not in our online store, so we export the lists from both systems. Since the lists do not have a common lookup field, we must make our comparison based on multiple columns. Three columns need to be inspected: class, subclass, and component.

When an item on the accounting system list is found in the online store list, we want to show a value of "Web", otherwise, "Missing." The list exported from the online store is placed in a table named *tbl_web*. The first class value is stored in *B12*, the subclass is in *C12*, and the component is in *D12*. The following formula works:

```
=IF(COUNTIFS(tbl_web[Class],B12,tbl_web[Subclass],C12,

    tbl_web[Component],D12)=0,"Missing","Web")
```

**Where:**

- **COUNTIFS(tbl_web[Class],B12,tbl_web[Subclass],C12,tbl_web[Component],D12)=0** is the first argument of the IF function and returns TRUE if the COUNTIFS function evaluates to zero—that is, if the item is not found in the online store list.

- **Where:**

    - **tbl_web[Class]** the first range to inspect, the class column.

- **B12** is the class of the item.

- **tbl_web[Subclass]** is the second range to inspect, the subclass column.

- **C12** is the subclass of the item.

- **tbl_web[Component]** is the third range to inspect, the component column.

- **D12** is the component of the item.

- **"Missing"** is the second argument of the IF function and is returned when COUNTIFS=0—that is, when the item is not found.

- **"Web"** is the third argument of the IF function and is returned when COUNTIFS does not equal 0—that is, when the item is found.

Once the formula is filled down, it is easy to identify which items are in our accounting system but not in our online store.

## CHAPTER CONCLUSION

We can use the COUNTIFS to easily perform multicolumn list comparisons.

# Chapter 14: Indentation

## SET UP

How do you indent labels in your worksheets? That is, how do you create a hierarchy in your reports and other worksheets? One common method is simply to tab over to the next column, which provides the structure illustrated in Figure 33 below.

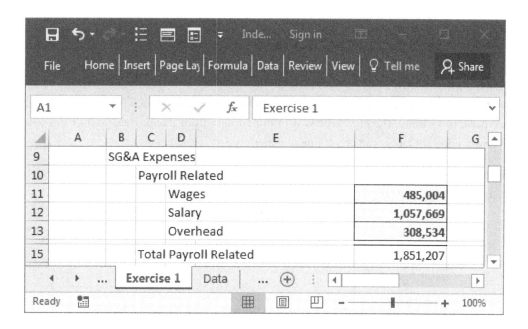

**Figure 33**

With this approach, a user simulates an indent by tabbing over one column to the right. This method simulates word processing, where you hit the Tab key to indent.

Another common method is preceding the cell value with two or more spaces, illustrated in Figure 34 below.

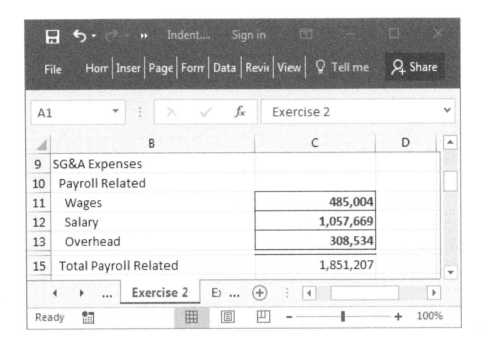

**Figure 34**

Neither of these methods promotes efficiency in recurring-use workbooks. This brings us to the reason why we are here: to examine the preferred way of indenting within Excel. Believe it or not, even a small detail like how we indent labels can affect our productivity.

To maximize efficiency for our formulas and lookup functions, the Indent button should be used to indent labels, as illustrated in Figure 35 below.

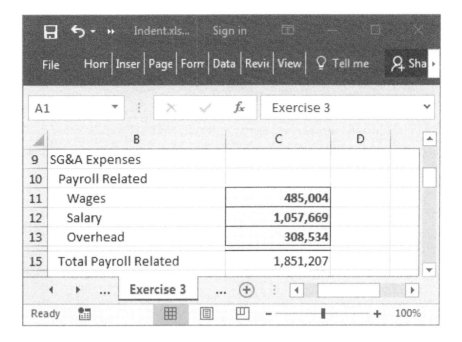

**Figure 35**

Not quite the revelation you were looking for, I know. But, when trying to maximize overall productivity, it is critical to be mindful of worksheet structure, including the way you indent. To be clear, we are not concerned about the time it takes to insert the indent; it is probably equally fast to insert an indent, hit Tab, or tap the space bar twice. The key benefit of using this approach is that you can fully use lookup functions, conditional summing functions, and anything else that requires labels to be stored in a single column consistently.

Let's unpack this. If I indent using the tab approach, it is difficult to write a formula that consistently retrieves values from this range. This is because I need to look for the label in multiple columns. The reverse also holds true: when I try to retrieve values from another range and pull them into my hierarchy, the lookup formula needs to deal with the fact that the label values reside in multiple columns.

Similar issues arise with the leading spaces approach. The lookup formulas won't match values between a list with leading spaces and a list without leading spaces. The lookup function breaks because the two cell values are not equal.

The indent approach enables us to use lookup formulas. Unlike the tab approach, it enables us to store all labels in a single column, making lookup formulas a breeze. Unlike the spaces approach, it ensures that the stored value matches the lookup value because it is not artificially padded with spaces. As you can see, the indent approach makes it easy to retrieve values both to and from this range.

## HOW TO

Excel has two indent command buttons: one increases the indent level and the other decreases the indent level. The command buttons are found on the Home tab and are displayed in Figure 36 below.

**Figure 36**

Use the following Ribbon command to increase the indent level of the cell value:

- Home > Increase Indent.

Use the following Ribbon command to decrease the indent level of the cell value:

- Home > Decrease Indent.

 **KB**

The keyboard shortcut I use to increase the indent is Alt+H, 6. To decrease the indent, I use Alt+H, 5.

Please note that if you click on the increase indent button multiple times, you will continue to increase the indent level.

## EXAMPLES

Let's explore the advantages by playing with some hands-on exercises.

 **PRACTICE**

To work along, please refer to *Indent.xlsx.*

**VIDEO**

To watch the solutions video, please visit the Excel University Video Library.

## EXERCISE 1—NEW COLUMN

In this exercise, we'll assess the effectiveness of simulating an indent by tabbing over to a new column.

 **PRACTICE**

To work along, please refer to the Exercise 1 worksheet.

Each month, we export data from our accounting system. We store the data in a table named *tbl_data*. We want to use the VLOOKUP function to build a report that will retrieve values from the table, based on the report labels.

We create the report hierarchy by tabbing over to the next column for various report labels.

The first account we want to retrieve is wages, and its label is stored in cell *D11*. We use the following formula to retrieve the wages value from the table:

```
=VLOOKUP(D11,tbl_data,2,0)
```

**Where:**

- **D11** is the lookup value.

- **tbl_data** is the lookup range.

- **2** is the column that has the value we want to return.

- **0** tells Excel we want to find an exact match.

This methodology works great for the first account. We quickly realize that we can't copy this formula down throughout the report range, because some labels are stored in column *D* while others are stored in column *E*. Populating this report requires two versions of the lookup formula: one version looks up the value in column *D* and the other version looks up the value in column *E*. This situation is no good for recurring-use workbooks, since to update the report we have to update multiple formulas. Since we prefer consistent formulas instead, it is clear that using multiple columns to simulate an indent is not very efficient.

## EXERCISE 2—SPACES

In this exercise, we'll assess the effectiveness of simulating an indent by using leading spaces.

 **PRACTICE**

> To work along, please refer to the Exercise 2 worksheet.

In this report, two leading spaces are used for each indent level. The stored values have been changed to include the leading spaces. Rather than containing the label such as "Wages," the stored value includes the leading spaces such as " Wages." The problem with this approach is that lookup functions won't match the account values.

To verify this, let's use the following formula to find the padded account label stored in *B11* in a table that contains account labels without leading spaces:

```
=VLOOKUP(B11,tbl_data,2,0)
```

**Where:**

- **B11** is the lookup value.
- **tbl_data** is the lookup range.
- **2** is the column that has the value we want to return.
- **0** tells Excel we want to find an exact match.

The formula returns an error because the values don't match. We determine that simulating an indent with leading spaces is not an effective approach when we need to use lookup formulas.

 **NOTE**

> While we prefer to use the indent command rather than leading spaces, please note that Excel contains the TRIM function, which will remove leading spaces. So, if you get in a pinch, feel free to wrap a TRIM function around the lookup value argument.

## EXERCISE 3—INDENT

In this exercise, we'll assess the effectiveness of using the indent command.

 **PRACTICE**

To work along, please refer to the Exercise 3 worksheet.

In this report, the accounts were indented with the indent command. The stored values are unchanged and do not contain leading spaces. All report labels are in column **B**, which allows us to use consistent formulas.

To verify this, we use the same lookup function as before:

```
=VLOOKUP(B11,tbl_data,2,0)
```

**Where:**

- **B11** is the lookup value.
- **tbl_data** is the lookup range.
- **2** is the column that has the value we want to return.
- **0** tells Excel we want to find an exact match.

When we copy the formula down throughout the report, we note that it continues to work for all accounts. Excellent! The conclusion is clear: for recurring-use workbooks that use lookup functions, the indent command is preferred.

Not only does this strategy work when we retrieve values into the report, as we've done in this exercise, but it also works when we retrieve values from the report. Let's check that out next.

## EXERCISE 4—HIGHLIGHTS

In this exercise, we'll retrieve values from a report containing properly indented labels.

 **PRACTICE**

To work along, please refer to the Exercise 4 worksheet.

In this worksheet, we want to retrieve values from a report. We will try to retrieve values from each of the three reports we set up during this chapter.

First, let's retrieve the values from the *Exercise 1* report, which used new columns to indent. A basic lookup formula works for the first cell, but it breaks when filled down. It breaks at the first account that is not found in the same lookup range column.

Next let's retrieve the values from the *Exercise 2* report, which used leading spaces to indent. A basic lookup formula can't make a match, since the stored values are different.

Finally, let's retrieve the values from the *Exercise 3* report, which used the indent command. A basic lookup formula works just fine throughout the range.

## EXERCISE 5—SELECTED ACCOUNTS

In this exercise we'll indent a report and confirm that the lookup formulas continue to work as expected.

 **PRACTICE**

> To work along please refer to the Exercise 5 worksheet.

In the exercises thus far, I set up the report structure and asked you write formulas to observe the results. In this exercise I wrote the formulas and will ask you to do the indenting.

Please indent the accounts on the exercise worksheet and ensure that the lookup formulas continue to work as expected.

## CHAPTER CONCLUSION

This chapter tries to demonstrate how important it is to structure data within worksheets to maximize productivity. Using the indent command is an example of this idea, and I hope you'll use it going forward.

# Chapter 15: Perform Lookups with SUMIFS

## SET UP

What is your favorite lookup function? Perhaps the most common answer is VLOOKUP. Other standard lookup functions include MATCH, INDEX, HLOOKUP, GETPIVOTDATA, and LOOKUP. Rarely is SUMIFS included in any list of lookup functions. In fact, Excel categorizes each function, and following is a list of all functions in the Lookup & Reference category:

- ADDRESS
- AREAS
- CHOOSE
- COLUMN
- COLUMNS
- GETPIVOTDATA
- HLOOKUP
- HYPERLINK
- INDEX
- INDIRECT
- LOOKUP

- MATCH

- OFFSET

- ROW

- ROWS

- RTD

- TRANSPOSE

- VLOOKUP

Not found in this list is SUMIFS. SUMIFS is typically referred to as a conditional summing function and is found in the Math & Trig function category.

SUMIFS can't perform all lookup tasks and is not appropriate in all situations. Recall that it returns a number, not a text string, so it couldn't be used to retrieve an account name. When the value we are trying to return is a number, such as an amount, it is a wonderful lookup function. We'll explore the advantages of using it to perform lookups.

## HOW TO

The SUMIFS function has the following structure:

```
=SUMIFS(sum_range, criteria_range1, criteria1,…)
```

**Where:**

- **sum_range** is the range that contains the cells to sum.

- **criteria_range1** is the first criteria range.

- **criteria1** is the first criteria value.

- **…** up to 127 total pairs.

The Excel developers designed the function with slightly different logic than was used in the traditional lookup functions. Let's identify the differences so that we can leverage them in our work. The key differences between the SUMIFS function and a traditional lookup function, such as VLOOKUP, include the following:

- **No match: No error.** When no matching value can be found, SUMIFS returns a zero, whereas VLOOKUP returns an error (assuming the fourth VLOOKUP argument is FALSE).

- **Returns: All matching items.** When the lookup value matches multiple rows in the lookup range, SUMIFS aggregates and returns the sum of all matching rows whereas VLOOKUP returns the related record from the first matching row.

- **Data types: Numbers match text strings.** While VLOOKUP does not match a numeric value of 100 to a text value of 100, the SUMIFS function will.

- **Return range: Dynamic.** Since the third argument of the VLOOKUP function is typically expressed as an integer rather than a range, a column inserted between the lookup and return columns breaks the VLOOKUP function. Since the SUMIFS function's arguments are expressed as range references, Excel can keep up with column inserts, and a column insert will not break the SUMIFS function.

These differences are summarized in Table 3 below.

| Item | VLOOKUP | SUMIFS |
|---|---|---|
| **No match**<br><br>If the lookup value is not found in the lookup range, what does the function return? | #N/A Error | 0 |
| **Returns**<br><br>If the lookup value is found on multiple rows in the lookup range, what does the function return? | The related value of the first matching row | The sum of all matching rows |
| **Data Types**<br><br>Will a numeric value match the equivalent text string? | Will not match | Will match |
| **Return Range**<br><br>If a user inserts a column between the lookup column and the return column, will the function break? | Will break | Will not break |

Table 3

# EXAMPLES

A few hands-on exercises are sure to demonstrate how the differences between traditional lookup and SUMIFS functions can be leveraged in our workbooks.

 **PRACTICE**

To work along, please refer to *Lookup with Sumifs.xlsx.*

 **VIDEO**

To watch the solutions video, please visit the Excel University Video Library.

## EXERCISE 1—RETURN ALL ITEMS

As you know, the SUMIFS function returns the sum of all matching items in the list, while the VLOOKUP function returns the related value of the first matching item. In this exercise we'll use the SUMIFS function to enhance a worksheet we previously prepared with VLOOKUP.

 **PRACTICE**

To work along, please refer to the Exercise 1 worksheet.

This worksheet was derived from the Chapter 5: Lookup Basics exercises, where we assumed that each account appeared only once in the data region. For this version of the exercise, I've added data so that each account appears multiple times within the data region. We'll see how VLOOKUP compares to SUMIFS.

First we try to retrieve the values from the table *tbl_data* for the account stored in cell *B14* with the following formula:

```
=VLOOKUP(B14,tbl_data,4,0)
```

**Where:**

- **B14** is the lookup value.

- **tbl_data** is the lookup range.

- **4** is the column number that has the value we want to return.

- **0** tells Excel we are not doing a range lookup.

When we fill the formula down and inspect the results, we notice that only the first matching item is returned. Since we want the sum of all matching items we instead use the following:

```
=SUMIFS(tbl_data[Amount],tbl_data[Account],B14)
```

**Where:**

- **tbl_data[Amount]** is the column of numbers to add.
- **tbl_data[Account]** is the criteria range.
- **B14** is the criteria value.

When we fill the formula down the sum of all matching items is returned, and this is perfect for our project!

## EXERCISE 2—NO MATCH ERRORS

In this exercise, we'll compare how VLOOKUP and SUMIFS behave when no match is found.

 **PRACTICE**

To work along, please refer to the Exercise 2 worksheet.

This worksheet was introduced in Chapter 9: Trap Errors with IFERROR, where we attempted to retrieve an amount from the current-month data into the report. At that time we wrapped the IFERROR around the VLOOKUP so that when an account was not found in the data, a zero would be returned rather than #N/A. This time we'll simplify our formula to use a single SUMIFS function.

The current-month data is stored in a table named *tbl_cm*. We want to retrieve the current-month data into our report. The first account, wages, is stored in cell *B14*.

To compare the difference between VLOOKUP and SUMIFS, we start by writing the following VLOOKUP function:

```
=VLOOKUP(B14,tbl_cm,2,0)
```

**Where:**

- **B14** is the lookup value.
- **tbl_cm** is the lookup range.

- **2** is the return column.

- **0** indicates exact match logic.

When we fill this formula down, we notice that anytime the account is not found in the current-month data, the VLOOKUP function returns #N/A error, which is ugly and corrupts our total formula. Now let's perform the same task with the following SUMIFS function:

```
=SUMIFS(tbl_cm[Amount],tbl_cm[Account],B14)
```

**Where:**

- **tbl_cm[Amount]** is the column of numbers to add.

- **tbl_cm[Account]** is the criteria range.

- **B14** is the criteria value.

When we fill this formula down, we notice that any time the account is not found in the current-month data, the SUMIS function returns zero. This looks better and does not corrupt our total formula. Fantastic!

## EXERCISE 3—DATA TYPES

In this exercise, we'll explore how different data types, such as numbers vs. text strings, trip up traditional lookup functions but not the SUMIFS function.

 **PRACTICE**

To work along, please refer to the Exercise 3 worksheet.

We need to retrieve an amount from a data range into our summary. We use the vendor ID field to perform the lookup. The vendor IDs at our company have different formats: some are alphanumeric, such as CCD075, and some are numeric, such as 40012. When we import data from our accounting system, the vendor ID field is interpreted as a text column, and all vendor IDs are stored as a text data type. However, when a user types in a vendor ID that contains all numerals, Excel stores it as a numeric data type. The fact that the vendor IDs are stored as different data types confuses Excel's traditional lookup functions.

To demonstrate this issue, let's start by using the VLOOKUP function to retrieve the amount from the *tbl_vendors* table. The first vendor ID is stored in cell *B14*. The following VLOOKUP function is used:

```
=VLOOKUP(B14,tbl_vendors,4,0)
```

**Where:**

- **B14** is the lookup value.

- **tbl_vendors** is the lookup range.

- **4** is the return column.

- **0** indicates exact match logic.

When we fill the formula down, we notice that it returns #N/A for those vendors where the vendor ID is stored as a numeric data type.

Let's try the following SUMIFS function and see how it behaves:

```
=SUMIFS(tbl_vendors[Amount],tbl_vendors[Vendor ID],B14)
```

**Where:**

- **tbl_vendors[Amount]** is the column of numbers to add.

- **tbl_vendors[Vendor ID]** is the criteria range.

- **B14** is the criteria value.

When we fill the formula down, we notice that it returns the expected amount for all vendors. It realizes that the vendor ID is a match even if it is stored as different data types.

If you ask me, this makes SUMIFS the preferred choice for our workbooks.

## EXERCISE 4—DYNAMIC RETURN RANGE

In this exercise we'll explore how the VLOOKUP and SUMIFS functions behave when a user inserts new columns into a worksheet.

 **PRACTICE**

To work along, please refer to the Exercise 4 worksheet.

We previously discussed another pitfall of the VLOOKUP function, which is the fact that it does not adapt when a new column is inserted between the lookup column and the return column. Let's see how the SUMIFS function behaves in this situation.

In this exercise we need to retrieve the amount from the data table named *tbl_v_data* into our summary based on the vendor ID. The first vendor ID in our summary is stored in *B14*. We write the following VLOOKUP formula to retrieve the amount:

```
=VLOOKUP(B14,tbl_v_data,4,0)
```

**Where:**

- **B14** is the lookup value.

- **tbl_v_data** is the lookup range.

- **4** is the return column number.

- **0** indicates exact match logic.

We fill the formula down, and everything looks good so far. Next let's retrieve the amount using the following SUMIFS function:

```
=SUMIFS(tbl_v_data[Amount],tbl_v_data[Vendor ID],B14)
```

**Where:**

- **tbl_v_data[Amount]** is the column of numbers to add.

- **tbl_v_data[Vendor ID]** is the criteria range.

- **B14** is the criteria value.

We fill the formula down, and everything looks good. Now let's compare how the formulas respond when a new column is inserted between the lookup column (*B*) and the return column (*E*).

When we insert a new column anywhere between columns *B* and *E*, we observe that the VLOOKUP function breaks, while the SUMIFS function continues to work as expected. This is simply because the VLOOKUP expresses the return column as an integer value rather than a range reference. Since the SUMIFS function automatically adapts to new column inserts, it tends to be more reliable for recurring-use workbooks.

## CHAPTER CONCLUSION

Consider using SUMIFS instead of traditional lookup functions when you need to return numbers. You'll probably discover that it works better for many tasks that you've historically accomplished with VLOOKUP. I hope that you continue to explore other creative ways to integrate the SUMIFS function into your workbooks; it is truly a gift from Microsoft. :-)

# DATE AND TEXT FUNCTION BASICS

*It is important to realize that Excel formulas are not limited to numbers.*

# Chapter 16: Determine the Last Day of the Month with EOMONTH

## SET UP

When we use Excel formulas to return and operate on numbers only, we miss opportunities to improve productivity. Excel is adept at working with various data types, including dates and text strings. By considering nonnumeric cells, we increase the number of cells that formulas can compute. This improves the efficiency of recurring-use workbooks.

If we reflect on the kinds of workbooks we set up, we realize that date values are often integral—for example, reports reflect activity for a given accounting period, transactions fall within a date range, and journal entries have a posting date. Since Excel includes many date functions, we can more fully automate these types of date-driven workbooks.

Let's get warmed up by exploring one of my favorite date functions, EOMONTH, which returns the last day of a month (End Of MONTH).

## HOW TO

Before we dig into the EOMONTH function, it is probably worth taking a moment to explore how Excel stores and processes dates.

What appears to the user as a date, for example 11/20/12, is the displayed value. The stored value is actually a number—for example, 41233. This number is commonly referred to as a date serial number or serial number. It is simply a running count of days, where 1 is equal to January 1, 1900, the earliest date recognized by Excel. You can easily view the serial number of any date by changing the cell format from a date format to general.

 **XREF**

Stored values and displayed values are discussed in Volume 1, Chapter 3.

 **NOTE**

If you are working with dates in the year 1900, note that Excel improperly treats it as a leap year. According to Microsoft, this was an intentional design consideration to ensure compatibility with other spreadsheet programs. Find more information here: http://support.microsoft.com/kb/214058.

This system allows Excel to store a single value and display it with a wide variety of date formats. While this is a fairly obvious advantage, a subtle benefit is date math. Since dates are essentially numbers, you are free to add and subtract them. For example, you can take a date and add 1 to return the next day or subtract two dates to determine the number of days between them. There are many ways to perform date calculations.

It is time to explore the EOMONTH function, which returns the last day of a month given a starting date.

This is the syntax for the EOMONTH function:

```
=EOMONTH(start_date, months)
```

**Where:**

- **start_date** is the starting date, expressed as a cell reference, serial number, or function.

- **months** is the number of months after the start_date expressed as an integer, positive for future periods, negative for prior periods, or 0 for the current period. For example, 0 for the last day in the start_date month, 1 for the next month, and -1 for the previous month.

Assume that start_date is equal to 1/1/2014. If months is equal to 0, then the function returns 1/31/2014, which represents the last day in the month of start_date. If months is equal to -1, then the function returns 12/31/2013, the last day in the previous month. If months is equal to 1, then the function returns 2/28/2014, which is the last day of the next month.

Table 4 below contains several examples for consideration. Please look at each formula and try to predict what it returns.

| Formula | Returns |
|---|---|
| When start_date = 1/1/2014 | |
| =EOMONTH(start_date,0) | 1/31/2014, the last day of the current month |
| =EOMONTH(start_date,0)+1 | 2/1/2014, the first day of the next month |
| =EOMONTH(start_date,1) | 2/28/2014, the last day of the next month |
| =EOMONTH(start_date,-1) | 12/31/2013, the last day of the previous month |
| =EOMONTH(start_date,-1)+1 | 1/1/2014, the first day of the current month |

Table 4

As you can see, the EOMONTH function makes it easy to compute both the first and last day of any given month. This ability can be leveraged when retrieving data into automated reports and in other date-driven worksheets.

## EXAMPLES

Let's get some hands-on practice by applying this function to some worksheets.

 **PRACTICE**

To work along, please refer to *Eomonth.xlsx.*

 **VIDEO**

To watch the solutions video, please visit the Excel University Video Library.

## EXERCISE 1—MONTH END

In this exercise, we'll compute the end of the month of a user-entered date.

 **PRACTICE**

To work along, please refer to the Exercise 1 worksheet.

Our goal is to compute the last day of the month of the date entered into the input cell **C8**.

The following EOMONTH function works perfectly:

`=EOMONTH(C8,0)`

**Where:**

- **C8** is the date that the function uses as the start date.

- **0** tells Excel to find the last day in the month of the start date.

Enter a few different dates into the input cell, and note that the EOMONTH function returns the expected results.

## EXERCISE 2—NAMED REFERENCES

In this exercise, we'll use the EOMONTH function to determine the first and last days of the month.

 **PRACTICE**

To work along, please refer to the Exercise 2 worksheet.

As you know, one of our goals when using Excel is to anticipate ways that a user can break our workbook. This design principle helps us create bulletproof workbooks that continue to function over time.

 **XREF**

Workbook design principles are discussed in Volume 1, Chapter 18.

In the first exercise, we entered the start period as a date and then used the EOMONTH function to determine the last day of the month. Excel allowed us to enter the first day of the month, such as 1/1/2014, but did not require it. We could have entered say 1/15/2014. The EOMONTH function simply returned the last day in the month of the date entered.

Let's assume for a moment that we had built some formulas that use the entered start date and the computed end date to create a report. The report is always supposed to reflect a full-month period, from the first day of the month to the last. If we entered a date other than the first day of a month, our report would be inaccurate, since it would only include a partial month.

Since one of our key workbook design principles is to create bulletproof workbooks, we try to address this risk up front. There are a couple of different approaches available. One approach is to use data validation to try to force the user to enter a date that represents the first day of the month. An easier approach is simply to allow the user to enter any date, compute the report start and end dates, and then use the computed dates in the report formulas. This is the approach we'll explore in this exercise.

 **XREF**

Data validation is discussed in Volume 1, Chapter 9.

To prepare the worksheet for use, name the user input cell *date_input*.

To compute the month start value, which is the first day in the month of the entered date, we use the following formula:

```
=EOMONTH(date_input,-1)+1
```

**Where:**

- **EOMONTH(date_input,-1)** returns the last day of the month prior to the user-entered date.

- **Where:**

    - **date_input** is the date entered by the user.

    - **-1** tells the function to compute the last day of the prior month.

- **+1** tells Excel to add one day to the date returned by the EOMONTH function, which returns the first day of the month of the user-entered date.

To compute the month end date, which is the last day of the month of the entered date, we use the following formula:

```
=EOMONTH(date_input,0)
```

**Where:**

- **date_input** is the user-entered date.

- **0** tells the function to return the last day in the month of the user-entered date.

The user can enter any date and our smart formulas compute the first and last days in that month. This type of approach helps us build bulletproof workbooks.

## EXERCISE 3—VARIOUS DATES

In this exercise, we'll use the EOMONTH function in a variety of formulas.

 **PRACTICE**

To work along, please refer to the Exercise 3 worksheet.

The user-entered date is stored in a cell named *date_user*. For the following formulas, assume the date entered is 1/1/2015.

**To return 1/31/2015**, we need to compute the last day of the month:

```
=EOMONTH(date_user,0)
```

**Where:**

- **date_user** is the user date, or 1/1/2015.

- **0** tells the function to return the last day in the month of the user date, or 1/31/2015.

**To return 2/1/2015**, we need to compute the day that follows the last day in the user date month:

```
=EOMONTH(date_user,0)+1
```

**Where:**

- **EOMONTH(date_user,0)** returns the last day in the month of the user date.

- **Where:**

  - **date_user** is the user date, or 1/1/2015.

  - **0** tells the function to return the end of the month of the user date, or 1/31/2015.

- **+1** adds one day to the results of the EOMONTH function to determine the first day of the next month, or 2/1/2015.

**To return 1/1/2016**, we need to compute the day that follows the last day of the month that is 11 months after the user-entered date:

```
=EOMONTH(date_user,11)+1
```

**Where:**

- **EOMONTH(date_user,11)** returns the last day of the month that is 11 months after the user date, since the user-entered date is a January date, 11 months after that is December.

- **Where:**

    - **date_user** is the user date, or 1/1/2015.

    - **11** tells the function to return the last day of the month that is 11 months after the user date, or 12/31/2015.

- **+1** tells Excel to add a day to the results of the EOMONTH function, or 1/1/2016.

**To return 3/31/2015**, we need to compute the last day of the month that is two months after the user-entered date:

```
=EOMONTH(date_user,2)
```

**Where:**

- **date_user** is the user date, or 1/1/2015.

- **2** tells the function to return the last day of the month that is two months after the user date, or 3/31/2015.

**To return 1/1/2014**, we want to compute the day that follows the last day of the month that is 13 months prior to the user date:

```
=EOMONTH(date_user,-13)+1
```

**Where:**

- **=EOMONTH(date_user,-13)** returns the last day of the month that is 13 months prior to the user date.

- **Where:**

  - **date_user** is the user date, or 1/1/2015.

    - **-13** tells the function to return the last day of the month that is 13 months prior to the user date, or 12/31/2013.

  - **+1** adds a day to the results of the EOMONTH function, which results in 1/1/2014.

**To return 12/31/2015**, we want to return the last day of the month that is 11 months after the user date:

```
=EOMONTH(date_user,11)
```

**Where:**

- **date_user** is the user date or 1/1/2015.

- **11** tells the function to return the last day of the month that is 11 months after the user date, or 12/31/2015.

Hopefully these examples help demonstrate how to use the EOMONTH function to achieve the date you need.

## EXERCISE 4—PERIOD TABLE

In this exercise, we'll set up a period table that computes the start and end dates in all months of a year.

 **PRACTICE**

To work along, please refer to the Exercise 4 worksheet.

We'll enter the first day of any year as a date. We need to develop formulas that set up our accounting periods for all months in the year. The idea is to generate a worksheet similar to Figure 37 below.

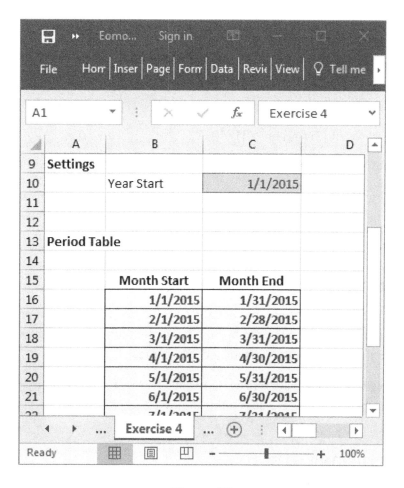

**Figure 37**

The year-start input cell is named ***year_start***. The formula to populate the January month start value is easy to create because it is just a cell reference to ***year_start***, which returns 1/1/2015. The formula to populate the January month-end cell is also easy to create, as we use a simple EOMONTH function to compute 1/31/2015:

```
=EOMONTH(B16,0)
```

**Where:**

- **B16** is the January start month date.

- **0** tells the function to return the last day of January.

The February month start value is also easily computed. We just need to add a day to the January month-end value and can use a simple formula:

```
=C16+1
```

**Where:**

- **C16** is the last day of January, or 1/31/2015.

- **+1** adds a day to 1/31/2015 to return 2/1/2015.

The February month-end value is easily computed with a simple EOMONTH function, similar to the formula used to compute the January month end value. The formulas used to compute the February row can simply be filled down throughout the remainder of the range, and we are done.

 **XREF**

> We strive to build worksheets that use the formula-consistency idea presented in Volume 1. There are several approaches to writing consistent formulas in this worksheet, one of which uses the ROW function, discussed in Volume 4, Chapter 11.

Since the period table is generated with formulas, it would be easy to enter a new date and have Excel instantly update the table for next year's accounting periods.

## CHAPTER CONCLUSION

Having the ability to easily compute the first and last days of a month is quite handy, and we'll revisit the EOMONTH function as we continue to develop hands-free reports.

# Chapter 17: Date Parts—MONTH and YEAR

## SET UP

It is sometimes helpful to be able to extract the month or year from any given date. Excel makes these tasks easy with the MONTH and YEAR functions.

While I typically use these functions as part of a larger formula, they can also be useful on their own. For example, they can generate a grouping column that is subsequently referenced in other formulas, reports, or objects.

In addition to returning the month and year parts of a date, Excel can also return the day with the DAY function. I use this function less frequently, so we'll focus on the MONTH and YEAR functions for the remainder of this chapter.

## HOW TO

Both the MONTH and YEAR functions have a single argument: the date. Given a date, the MONTH function returns the month number of the date, such as 1 for January or 12 for December. The YEAR function returns the year of the date.

Here is the syntax for the MONTH function:

```
=MONTH(serial_number)
```

**Where:**

- **serial_number** is a date serial number, often expressed as a cell reference.

This is the syntax for the YEAR function:

```
=YEAR(serial_number)
```

**Where:**

- **serial_number** is a date serial number, often expressed as a cell reference.

# EXAMPLES

We'll get some practice using these functions.

 **PRACTICE**

To work along, please refer to **Date Parts.xlsx.**

 **VIDEO**

To watch the solutions video, please visit the Excel University Video Library.

### EXERCISE 1—MONTH

In this exercise, we'll populate a month column and use the results in a summary function.

 **PRACTICE**

To work along, please refer to the Exercise 1 worksheet.

In this worksheet, we paste values from our accounting system into the table named *tbl_data*. The transactions span many months. For a particular monthly report, we need to summarize a subset of all of the transactions—namely, all of the transactions for a specified month.

Again, as with almost anything in Excel, there are several ways to handle this task. One approach is to set up a helper column that computes the month for each transaction and then to use a conditional summing function, such as SUMIFS, to aggregate the transactions for the desired month. This is the approach we'll discuss now, but we'll be discussing an approach that eliminates the need for this helper column in a subsequent chapter of this volume. And we'll discuss the PivotTable approach in Volume 3.

 **XREF**

Using the SUMIFS without a helper column will be discussed in Chapter 20: Improve SUMIFS with CONCATENATE.

 **XREF**

PivotTables are discussed in Volume 3.

We'll use the MONTH function to build the helper column that defines the groups and add it as a new column to our table.

First, we'll automatically expand the table for our new column by typing the column header "Month" into the cell immediately to the right of the amount column header. Then we'll write the formula for the month column in the first row of the table:

```
=MONTH([@Date])
```

**Where:**

- **[@Date]** is the cell that contains the date, the structured table reference for the date column.

 **NOTE**

Depending on which version of Excel you are using, the structured table reference [@ Date] can also be expressed as [Date].

The table automatically fills the formula down, leaving us with a column that contains the month number of all transactions, as shown in Figure 38 below.

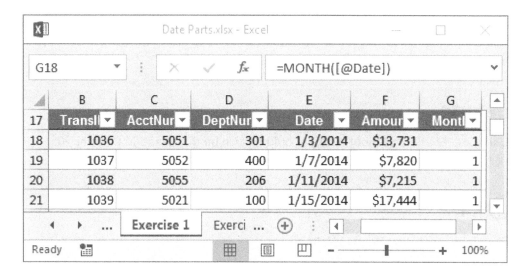

**Figure 38**

Summing the amount for any desired month is now pretty easy. If we want to add up all January transactions, we just sum the amount column for all rows where the month is equal to 1. We can easily accomplish this with our favorite conditional summing function, SUMIFS.

Assuming the desired month number is stored in cell *B12*, the following formula does the trick:

```
=SUMIFS(tbl_data[Amount],tbl_data[Month],B12)
```

**Where:**

- **tbl_data[Amount]** is the column of numbers to add, the amount column.

- **tbl_data[Month]** is the criteria column, the month column.

- **B12** is the criteria value, the cell that contains the desired month number.

Having the ability to pull out date parts is handy, and it makes it easy to sum groups of transactions.

## EXERCISE 2—YEAR

In this exercise, we'll populate a year column.

 **PRACTICE**

To work along, please refer to the Exercise 2 worksheet.

We want to paste fixed asset purchase transactions from our accounting system into the table named *tbl_fa*. The transactions span many years. For a particular report, we need to summarize a subset of all the transactions—namely, all transactions for a specified year.

To begin, we'll add a table column header (Year) by typing it into the column to the right of the amount column. This should automatically expand the table to include the new column. Next we'll write the following formula to compute the values:

```
=YEAR([@Date])
```

**Where:**

- **[@Date]** is the structured reference to the date value.

When the formula is entered in the first row, Excel automatically fills the formula down, creating a column with the year of each transaction.

Creating the summary is easy. We simply rely on our good friend SUMIFS. Assuming that the desired year is stored in cell *B12*, the following formula will sum all transactions for the year:

```
=SUMIFS(tbl_fa[Amount],tbl_fa[Year],B12)
```

**Where:**

- **tbl_fa[Amount]** is the column of numbers to add, the amount column.

- **tbl_fa[Year]** is the criteria range, the year column.

- **B12** is the criteria value, the desired year.

Now we have a total of all transactions that occurred within the specified year.

## CHAPTER CONCLUSION

The ability to extract date parts from a date value is handy, especially when working with date-driven workbooks and reports.

# Chapter 18: Build Your Own Date with DATE

## SET UP

When working with date-driven workbooks and reports, we can automate certain tasks by building our own date values that can be displayed or used as function arguments. The DATE function enables us to build a date.

## HOW TO

The DATE function returns a valid Excel date serial when given the year, month, and day. Here is the syntax for the DATE function:

```
=DATE(year, month, day)
```

**Where:**

- **year** is the year of the date to return.

- **month** is the month number of the date to return.

- **day** is the day number of the date to return.

If you need the date serial for January 15, 2014, you can use the following function:

```
=DATE(2014,1,15)
```

**Where:**

- **2014** is the year of the date to return.

- **1** is the month of the date to return.

- **15** is the day of the date to return.

This function returns the Excel date serial 41654, which represents 1/15/2014. When returned to a cell, the date serial adopts the date formatting of the cell and appears as a date.

This function has a bit of subtle logic. For the month and day arguments, the function actually supports values that are greater or less than valid date entries. When an argument value is greater than a valid date entry, Excel adds the increment to the calculated date. When an argument value is less than a valid date entry, Excel subtracts that amount from the calculated date. For example, there are 12 months in a year, but the function supports month arguments of greater than 12 and less than 1. If you enter a month argument value of 13, then Excel adds one, basically advancing forward to January of the *next year*. Values of less than 1 similarly roll back to previous months.

The day argument works the same way. If a day value is greater than the number of days in the month, Excel adds that excess to the computed date. If a day value of less than 1 is used, Excel backs up the date accordingly, where a day value of 0 backs up the returned date by one day. Setting the day value to 0, so that the function returns the previous day, makes it an alternative to the EOMONTH function to determine the last day of a month.

I think a table of examples may help. Please check out the various functions in Table 5.

| Function | Returns |
|---|---|
| =DATE(2014,1,15) | 1/15/2014 |
| =DATE(2014,2,22) | 2/22/2014 |
| =DATE(2014,13,1) | 1/1/2015 |
| =DATE(2014,1,1) | 1/1/2014 |
| =DATE(2014,1,0) | 12/31/2013 |

**Table 5**

Please note that when the argument value is greater than or less than a valid month or day value, Excel actually advances the whole date, not just the argument, forward or backward—that is, a month entry of 13 advances the returned date by one year.

## EXAMPLES

Let's get some hands-on practice now.

 **PRACTICE**

To work along, please refer to *Date.xlsx.*

 **VIDEO**

To watch the solutions video, please visit the Excel University Video Library.

## EXERCISE 1—WARM UP

In this exercise, we'll just get warmed up.

 **PRACTICE**

To work along, please refer to the Exercise 1 worksheet.

Our objective is to create a formula that returns the first day of the calendar year specified by the user. For example, if the user enters 2010 for the year, then our formula should return 1/1/2010.

Assuming that the user enters the year into cell *C8*, then the following formula produces the desired result:

```
=DATE(C8,1,1)
```

**Where:**

- **C8** is the year argument, the user-entered year.

- **1** is month 1, or January.

- **1** is day 1.

Now that you are warmed up, let's move on to something more interesting.

## EXERCISE 2—FIRST DAY

In this exercise, we'll prepare a helper column that contains a date value.

 **PRACTICE**

To work along, please refer to the Exercise 2 worksheet.

In this worksheet, we need to build a report from a table named *tbl_data*. The table stores transactions, and each transaction has a date. We want to build a report that sums up all transactions within a given month. Although there are many ways to approach this task, we'll create a new calculated date field (Period) that reflects the first day of the transaction month. For example, if the transaction date is 1/22/2014, then the period value should be 1/1/2014. This way all transactions for a given month are assigned with the same period value, making it easy to build a summary report using SUMIFS.

The first step is to build the period field in the table. This can be accomplished with a DATE function combined with nested MONTH and YEAR functions:

```
=DATE(YEAR([@Date]),MONTH([@Date]),1)
```

**Where:**

- **YEAR([@Date])** returns the year of the transaction.

- **Where:**

  - [@Date] refers to the value found at the intersection of the current row and the date column.

- **MONTH([@Date])** returns the month of the transaction.

- **Where:**

  - [@Date] refers to the value found at the intersection of the current row and the date column.

- **1** indicates day 1.

When we hit Enter, the formula is automatically filled down, and we are looking good.

Next we need to build the report formulas with the SUMIFS function. Assuming the first period desired is stored in cell *B12*, then the following formula produces the desired result:

```
=SUMIFS(tbl_data[Amount],tbl_data[Period],B12)
```

**Where:**

- **tbl_data[Amount]** is the column of numbers to add, the amount column.

- **tbl_data[Period]** is the criteria range, the period column.

- **B12** is the criteria, the date value that represents the period.

We can fill this formula down through the report—and bam, we're done.

This structure is beautiful. Since the transaction data is stored in a table, we can easily append new transactions. Since the period field is calculated, Excel automatically fills it down through all new rows. And since the summary report was built on a date value rather than just a month part, only the period of the year desired will be aggregated, even if the transactions span multiple years. This approach is fairly solid and works well in practice. One disadvantage of this setup is that we use a helper column—that is, the period column. In a subsequent chapter we'll explore an approach that eliminates the need for a helper column.

 **XREF**

Using SUMIFS without a helper column will be discussed in Chapter 20: Improve SUMIFS with CONCATENATE.

## EXERCISE 3—ALTERNATIVE TO EOMONTH

In this exercise, we'll simulate the capability of the EOMONTH function with the DATE function.

 **PRACTICE**

To work along, please refer to the Exercise 3 worksheet.

In this worksheet we want the user to enter any date into the input cell **C9**. We want to write formulas that return the first day of the month of the date entered, as well as the last day of the month. Obtaining the first day of the month is relatively straightforward and can be computed with the following formula:

```
=DATE(YEAR(C9),MONTH(C9),1)
```

**Where:**

- **YEAR(C9)** returns the year of the entered date.

- **Where:**

    - **C9** is the date entered by the user.

- **MONTH(C9)** returns the month of the entered date.

- **Where:**

    - **C9** is the date entered by the user.

- **1** sets the day equal to one.

The next value to compute is the last day of the month. In a previous chapter, we explored how to accomplish this with the EOMONTH function; however, we can also compute the last day of the month with the DATE function.

 **XREF**

The EOMONTH function is discussed in Chapter 16: Determine the Last Day of the Month with EOMONTH.

As we know, the DATE function has three arguments: year, month, and day. As discussed previously, passing a 0 for the day argument actually subtracts one day from the date that would have been produced assuming a day of 1—that is, when 0 is entered for the day argument, Excel returns the last day of the previous month. For example, the following formula returns the last day of the month of the entered date:

```
=DATE(YEAR(C9),MONTH(C9)+1,0)
```

**Where:**

- **YEAR(C9)** returns the year of the entered date.

- **Where:**

    - **C9** is the date entered by the user.

- **MONTH(C9)+1** returns the month that follows the entered date (if the entered date is December, this advances forward to January of the next year).

- **Where:**

    - **C9** is the date entered by the user.

- **0** tells the function to back up one day, to the last day of the previous month.

Using either EOMONTH or DATE to compute the last day of any month helps us automate date-driven worksheets and reports.

## CHAPTER CONCLUSION

As you can see, generating a valid date serial with the DATE function allows us to build a date. When combined with date part functions like YEAR and MONTH, the DATE function helps us automate our work.

# Chapter 19: Concatenation Basics

## SET UP

Excel formulas can operate on a variety of data types, including numbers, dates, and text strings. The ability to join, or concatenate, text values to create a single text string is surprisingly handy, especially when developing hands-free reports.

As you well know, I like to delegate as many cells to Excel as possible, and that, by definition, means converting value cells into formula cells. We've spent the past few chapters discussing various functions that operate on date values. In this chapter, we'll discuss one of the key text-based functions, CONCATENATE.

The idea behind CONCATENATE is simple: it joins multiple text values and returns a single text value. As a simple example, if the cell *A1* contains the value "Excel" and *B1* contains the value "University" then we could write a formula that concatenates them and returns the phrase "Excel University." This is the basic idea behind concatenation, but as we'll see shortly, this simple idea contains many practical applications.

## HOW TO

The CONCATENATE function returns a text string that combines all of its arguments. The syntax for the function is straightforward:

```
=CONCATENATE(text1, [text2], …)
```

**Where:**

- **text1** is a cell reference, text value, or function.

- **[text2]** optional cell reference, text value, or function.

- **...** additional arguments (the function supports up to 255 total arguments).

 **NOTE**

Arguments expressed as text values need to be enclosed in quotation marks.

In addition to the CONCATENATE function to combine values, you can use the concatenation operator: the ampersand (&). Building a formula with the concatenation operator is easy; you just place the ampersand between the text strings. In a way, the ampersand is the analog to the addition operator (+), but instead of adding numbers, you are joining text strings. In a formula, you just place the operator between the values as follows:

```
=text1&text2
```

**Where:**

- **text1** is expressed as a cell reference, text value, or function.

- **text2** is expressed as a cell reference, text value, or function.

It is simply a matter of personal preference as to which method you use. We'll use both in our exercises.

## EXAMPLES

Let's get a little practice.

 **PRACTICE**

To work along, please refer to *Concatenate.xlsx.*

 **VIDEO**

To watch the solutions video, please visit the Excel University Video Library.

## EXERCISE 1—TEXT

In this exercise, we'll get warmed up by concatenating first and last names.

 **PRACTICE**

To work along, please refer to the Exercise 1 worksheet.

In this worksheet we store a list of employees exported from our payroll system. The payroll system exports the first and last names in separate columns. For our project, we need to combine these names into a single column. In fact we need to present them as: last name, first name. This sounds like a job for concatenation.

 **NOTE**

Beginning with Excel 2013, this task can also be accomplished manually with the Flash Fill feature.

The first employee's first name is in cell **B14**, and the last name is in **C14**. Thus the following formula does the trick:

```
=CONCATENATE(C14,", ",B14)
```

**Where:**

- **C14** is the last name.

- **", "** is the comma and space surrounded by quotes. Since this argument is expressed as a text string, it must be enclosed in quotes.

- **B14** is the first name.

Fill the formula down, and now we've got it.

To explore how to concatenate using the concatenation operator, use the following formula:

```
=C14&", "&B14
```

**Where:**

- **C14** is the last name.

- **&** is the concatenation operator.

- **", "** is the comma and space enclosed in quotes.

- **&** is the concatenation operator.

- **B14** is the first name.

Fill the formula down, and bam, we've got it.

For the remainder of the exercises, feel free to use either the CONCATENATE function or concatenation operator (&), based on your personal preference. This text will display the answers using the CONCATENATE function.

## EXERCISE 2—NUMBER

In this exercise, we'll concatenate numbers.

 **PRACTICE**

To work along, please refer to the Exercise 2 worksheet.

Let's say our accounting system exported a partial chart of accounts, and the three account number components—unit, department, and account—were split into three separate columns. For our project, we need to combine these values into a single column separated with a dash (-). For example, if the unit is 10, the department is 101, and the account is 10100, then the combined value we need in our cell is 10-101-10100.

The first unit value is in cell *B13*, the department value is in *C13*, and the account is in *D13*. The following formula does the trick:

```
=CONCATENATE(B13,"-",C13,"-",D13)
```

**Where:**

- **B13** is the unit value.

- **"-"** is the dash enclosed in quotes.

- **C13** is the department value.

- **"-"** is the dash enclosed in quotes.

- **D13** is the account number.

Fill the formula down, and we're done.

## EXERCISE 3—DATE

In this exercise, we'll concatenate a date value.

 **PRACTICE**

To work along, please refer to the Exercise 3 worksheet.

The user can enter a report date into an input cell, which formulas use to prepare the report headers. In this simple example, the input cell and the report label are on one sheet. In practice, however, the input cell might be stored on a Start Here worksheet.

 **XREF**

The Start Here worksheet is discussed in Volume 1, Chapter 15.

The report date input cell is named *date_rpt*, and the header text input cell is named *hdr_rpt*. The input cells are shown in Figure 39 below.

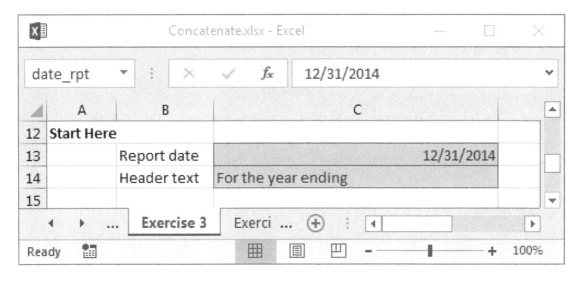

**Figure 39**

We want to write a formula that combines the header text and report date so we can use the combined string as a report label. We begin by simply concatenating the header text, a space, and the report date, as follows:

```
=CONCATENATE(hdr_rpt," ",date_rpt)
```

**Where:**

- **hdr_rpt** is the header text input cell.

- **" "** is a space enclosed in quotes.

- **date_rpt** is the report date input cell.

This formula, however, produces an unexpected result, as shown Figure 40 below.

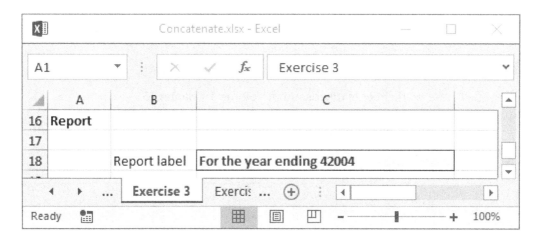

Figure 40

As you can see, the CONCATENATE function retrieved the report date, but the formula result displays the date as a serial number, not a date-formatted value. This is because the CONCATENATE function, like other worksheet functions, operates on the stored value, not the displayed value.

 **XREF**

The difference between stored and displayed values is discussed in Volume 1, Chapter 3.

Thus we need to convert this serial number into a value that is formatted as a date. Can you think of a worksheet function that accepts a numeric value and converts it to a formatted text string? Come on, be there for me.

Yes, the TEXT function! Good memory.

**XREF**

The TEXT function is discussed in Chapter 7: Improve VLOOKUP with VALUE and TEXT.

As you know, the TEXT function accepts a number as its first argument and converts the number into a text value according to the format code in the second argument. The idea here is to wrap a TEXT function around the report date to define the desired format.

The TEXT function supports a variety of formatting codes. For example, m returns the month number without a leading zero, mm returns the month number with a leading zero when necessary, mmm returns the three-letter month abbreviation, and mmmm returns the month name fully spelled out. Table 6 presents a few examples of date format codes applied to the value that represents January 1, 2014.

| Format code | Example result |
|---|---|
| **mm/dd/yy** | 01/01/14 |
| **mm/dd/yyyy** | 01/01/2014 |
| m/d/yy | 1/1/14 |
| **m** | 1 |
| **mm** | 01 |
| **mmm** | Jan |
| **mmmm** | January |
| **mmmm d, yyyy** | January 1, 2014 |
| **mmm-yyyy** | Jan-2014 |

**Table 6**

 **NOTE**

You can find more codes in the Excel help system and also by playing with the Custom codes in the Format Cells dialog box.

It is now easy to convert the date value into a text string with the proper date formatting and then use the result with the report header text. The following formula gets us there:

```
=CONCATENATE(hdr_rpt," ",TEXT(date_rpt,"mmmm dd, yyyy"))
```

**Where:**

- **hdr_rpt** is the header text.

- **" "** is a space enclosed in quotes.

- **TEXT(date_rpt,"mmmm dd, yyyy")** formats the date.

- **Where:**

  - **date_rpt** is the report date.

  - **"mmmm dd, yyyy"** is the formatting code to apply.

The result of this formula is shown in Figure 41 below.

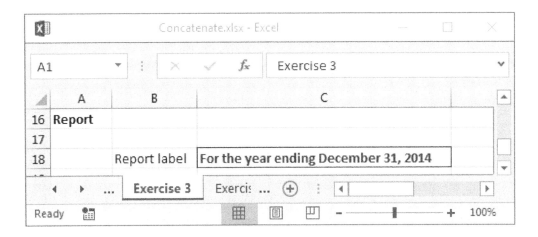

**Figure 41**

Now that we have this set up, we can update the report date in the input cell, and the report header formulas will be updated immediately.

I use this approach in many of my report workbooks. I know that once I enter the report date, all report headers reflect the proper date, and I don't need to manually update each report's header. I hope this approach provides efficiency to your workbooks.

## EXERCISE 4—CURRENCY

In this exercise, we'll concatenate some money.

 **PRACTICE**

To work along, please refer to the Exercise 4 worksheet.

We want to indicate the cash balance in our management summary. We obtain the cash balance from a cell named *cash_bal*. The summary should contain this specific language and formatting: "The cash balance is $#,###" with no decimals.

This sounds like a job for the CONCATENATE and TEXT functions. Thus we write the following formula:

```
=CONCATENATE("The cash balance is ",TEXT(cash_bal,"$#,###"))
```

**Where:**

- **"The cash balance is "** is the first text string to join, and it includes a trailing space.

- **TEXT(cash_bal, "$#,###")** returns the cash balance formatted as a currency.

- **Where:**

    - **cash_bal** is the cash balance input cell.

    - **"$#,###"** is the formatting code to apply to the value, currency, with symbol, no decimal.

 **NOTE**

A convenient alternative to the TEXT function when working specifically with dollar values is the DOLLAR function. Feel free to check it out within the Excel help system.

In practice, the cash balance may not be an input cell. It may be computed or stored on another worksheet. A single summary sheet could be set up to retrieve and store values from various workbook locations to be used in the report.


## CHAPTER CONCLUSION

The ability to concatenate text strings becomes increasingly important as we seek to delegate tasks to Excel. Since our overall goal is to convert manual input cells to formula cells, we love being able to compute text and date cells.

# HANDS-FREE REPORTING

*My favorite reports are hands-free.*

# Chapter 20: Improve SUMIFS with CONCATENATE

## SET UP

Up to this point we have discussed the mechanics needed to prepare hands-free reports. The next several chapters combine the individual items presented previously and expand their application.

Let's start by nesting the SUMIFS and CONCATENATE functions to see what we can accomplish.

 **XREF**

SUMIFS is discussed in Chapter 3: Conditional Summing Basics with SUMIFS.

 **XREF**

CONCATENATE is discussed in Chapter 19: Concatenation Basics.

As you know, SUMIFS is one of my favorite functions. Up until now, we've only been able to get partial utility out of it because we've not yet explored a critical capability. It is time to leverage the fact that it supports comparison arguments. We'll use concatenated strings to create some remarkable formulas.

# HOW TO

To briefly recap, the SUMIFS function's arguments go something like this: add up a column of numbers and only include those rows where the criteria range equals the criteria value. For example, add up the amount column, but only include those rows where the department column is equal to finance.

Up to this point, we've only considered using SUMIFS to add up cells where the criteria range is equal to the criteria value. This is a big deal, so I'll say it again.

> *We have only used the SUMIFS function to conditionally sum values where the criteria range is* **equal to** *the criteria value.*

The SUMIFS function supports wildcards and comparison operators in the criteria arguments. This is a huge benefit, and it lets us write some very cool formulas.

Here is a simple example: we can ask it to add up the amount column but only include those rows where the account number is greater than 500. Or we can ask it to add up the amount column but only include those rows where the amount is less than $5,000. Or we can ask it to add up the amount column but only include those rows where the date is greater than 1/1/2014.

Since SUMIFS is designed to handle multiple conditions, we could add up the amount column but only include those rows where the date column is greater than or equal to 1/1/2014 and where the date column is less than or equal to 1/31/2014.

In practice I frequently use comparison operators on date values, so this chapter's illustrations will be about date values. But I do want to point out that the SUMIFS function supports comparison operators and wildcards on other data types as well, including numbers, dollars, and text values. Please feel free to experiment with these other data types and explore the Excel help system for additional information.

The syntax for integrating a comparison operator within a SUMIFS function is, unfortunately, not simple. The good news is that you already have the skills needed and the required functions have been covered previously.

Essentially, we need to build a text string that contains the comparison operator along with the criteria value and use that whole string as the function argument.

To get warmed up, let's say we want to add up the amount column but only include those rows where the account number is greater than 500. Here is the criteria value argument of the SUMIFS function:

```
">500"
```

Since the argument is a text string, it is enclosed in quotes. If we want to include those rows where the account number is greater than or equal to 500, we use this:

```
">=500"
```

However, rather than hard code the criteria value inside of the text string, it is most beneficial to reference the cell that contains it. For example, if the value stored in cell *A1* is 500, then we use the following string for the criteria argument:

```
">="&A1
```

 **NOTE**

The idea of storing a variable in a cell and then referencing the cell in your formula or function is key in recurring-use workbooks. This approach is preferred to hard coding the value in the formula. In future periods, you can easily change the variable value by typing it into a cell, rather than needing to update all of the related formulas.

Notice the comparison operator is placed inside quotes and is followed by the concatenation operator (&) and the cell reference. Excel first converts the cell reference *A1* into its value and then concatenates the comparison operator and the value to pass the following text string to the SUMIFS function effectively:

```
">=500"
```

If you prefer the CONCATENATE worksheet function, you can use the following:

```
CONCATENATE(">=",A1)
```

 **NOTE**

It is simply a matter of personal preference whether to use the CONCATENATE worksheet function or the concatenation operator (&). My personal preference is to use the concatenation operator within SUMIFS functions, so this text will use that convention going forward, but feel free to use either method.

The same logic applies to date values. For example, if we want to write a SUMIFS function to add up the amount column but only include those rows where the transaction date is greater than or equal to the date stored in cell *B15*, the following can be used:

```
">="&B15
```

Got it? Good, it's time to jump into Excel.

## EXAMPLES

Let's get some hands-on practice.

 **PRACTICE**

To work along, please refer to *Sumifs with Concatenate.xlsx.*

 **VIDEO**

To watch the solutions video, please visit the Excel University Video Library.

## EXERCISE 1—MONTH

Let's get warmed up with a monthly report example.

 **PRACTICE**

To work along, please refer to the Exercise 1 worksheet.

The user enters a date into a cell. We write formulas to compute the first and last days of the month. We then use a SUMIFS function to compute the total of all transactions that fall between these two endpoints. If the user changes the date, the endpoints and total are immediately recomputed.

We had a similar task in the date parts chapter, and the way we accomplished it was to add a helper column to the table that computed the month. This time we'll accomplish the same task without the helper column. The approach presented here is preferred, since it requires no modification to the data table—namely, we don't need to add a helper column. Whenever possible, we prefer to leave the underlying data source in its original format. Remember, we want to work with the data as it comes to us.

 **XREF**

This task was accomplished by adding a helper column in Chapter 17: Date Parts—MONTH and YEAR.

The transactions are stored in a table named *tbl_data,* and the report date input cell is named *date_rpt*.

Computing the report start date is easy. The start date is the first day of the month of the report date. For example, if the user entered 1/1/2014, or even 1/15/2014, then the start date is 1/1/2014, the first day of the month.

The following formula should easily handle this task:

```
=EOMONTH(date_rpt,-1)+1
```

**Where:**

- **EOMONTH(date_rpt,-1)** returns the last day of the month that precedes the *date_rpt* date.

  - **Where:**

    - **date_rpt** is the report date.

    - **-1** tells the EOMONTH function to go back one month.

- **+1** adds one day to the last day of the prior month, resulting in the first day of the month of the entered date.

We can easily compute the last day of the month as follows:

```
=EOMONTH(date_rpt,0)
```

**Where:**

- **date_rpt** is the report date.

- **0** tells the function to return the last day of the month.

Now that we have computed the report's start and end dates, our final task is to sum up all transactions that fall on or within these two dates. This is where we use a SUMIFS function and comparison operators in the arguments.

The start date cell is named *date_start*, and the end date cell is named *date_end*. The following function does the trick:

```
=SUMIFS(tbl_data[Amount],
tbl_data[Date],">="&date_start,
```

```
tbl_data[Date],"<="&date_end)
```

**Where:**

- **tbl_data[Amount]** is the column of numbers to add, the amount column.

- **tbl_data[Date]** is the first criteria range, the date column.

- **">="&date_start** is the first criteria value, the concatenation of the greater than or equal to comparison operator and the start date.

- **tbl_data[Date]** is the second criteria range, the date column.

- **"<="&date_end** is the second criteria value, the concatenation of the less than or equal to comparison operator and the end date.

Take a moment to think about the fact that we used the date column in two criteria pairs. Since the SUMIFS function works with AND logic, then the row must contain a date that is both greater than or equal to the start date AND less than or equal to the end date.

 **NOTE**

> When using date values in SUMIFS arguments, storing the date in a cell and then referencing the cell is generally easier than entering a date serial directly.

If we now change the date input cell value in our worksheet, we notice that new start and end dates are computed, and a new total is computed. Excel rules!

## EXERCISE 2—YEAR

In this exercise, we'll compute a total for a year.

 **PRACTICE**

> To work along, please refer to the Exercise 2 worksheet.

The idea here is to allow the user to enter a year and then compute a total for the year. In a previous chapter we tackled this by adding a helper column to compute the year of each transaction. Then we used the SUMIFS function to add up all rows for the desired year. This time around we'll perform the same task without adding a helper column.

 **XREF**

> This task was accomplished by adding a helper column in Chapter 17: Date Parts—MONTH and YEAR.

The fixed asset transactions are stored in a table named *tbl_fa,* and the year input cell is named *date_year*.

We'll of course use the SUMIFS function to compute the total. Let's think about what we want the function to do. First, we want it to add up the amount column. Easy enough. Next we want it to include only those transactions where the date falls within January 1 of the entered year and December 31 of the entered year. Do we know a formula that, given the year, can return a date that is equal to the first day of that year? Come on, be there for me. Yes! The DATE function. The DATE function can just as easily compute the last day of the year.

 **XREF**

> The DATE function is discussed in Chapter 18: Build Your Own Date with DATE.

The following formula should do the trick for us:

```
=SUMIFS(tbl_fa[Amount],

tbl_fa[Date],">="&DATE(date_year,1,1),

tbl_fa[Date],"<="&DATE(date_year,12,31))
```

**Where:**

- **tbl_fa[Amount]** is the column of numbers to add, the amount column.

- **tbl_fa[Date]** is the first criteria range, the date column.

- **">="&DATE(date_year,1,1)** returns the concatenation of the greater than or equal to comparison operator and the date that is January 1 of the year entered by the user.

- **tbl_fa[Date]** is the second criteria range, again, the date column.

- **"<="&DATE(date_year,12,31)** returns the concatenation of the less than or equal to comparison operator and the date that is December 31 of the year entered by the user.

Now enter a different year, and the total should be recomputed instantly. Yummy!

## CHAPTER CONCLUSION

As you can see, the SUMIFS function is quite remarkable and has astounding utility. The ability to concatenate comparison operators and cell values enables us to write some incredible formulas. I use the same approach discussed in this chapter in my real-world workbooks, and I hope you find great use in your workbooks as well.

# Chapter 21: Dynamic Headers

## SET UP

How do you set up a report's headers when you need one column for each month? Do you enter the month names as text strings—for example, January, February, March, and so on? An example of this approach is shown in Figure 42 below.

| B | C | D |
|---|---|---|
| **January** | **February** | **March** |
| 20,156 | 25,811 | 21,115 |

Figure 42

Instead, perhaps you enter a date value, such as 1/1/2014, and then format it to hide the day, for example, Jan-2014.

These are likely the two most common ways to set up monthly column headers—but they shouldn't be. Well, at least they shouldn't be when our goal is to create hands-free reports in recurring-use workbooks.

When we are trying to get more done in less time, we want to eliminate manually entered cells and convert them to formulas. This overarching principle causes us to adopt certain approaches. Manually entering the column headers, whether they are text or date values, is not in line with our goal of hands-free reporting, and a couple of problems occur. Any cell that is manually entered will likely need to be reentered next period or next year, especially when date values are used. If a text string is used, such as January, it is more difficult to use it as a function argument. Both of these problems impede our productivity in recurring-use workbooks.

With hands-free reporting we want to enter a date in an input cell and have the report update not only the values but also the report labels and headers. This is the basic idea of dynamic headers: using formulas to populate report headers when it makes sense. Let's see how this works.

## HOW TO

Creating dynamic headers is pretty easy. In fact, you already have the skills needed and know the functions required.

The first thing to recognize is the usefulness of using date values rather than text labels. This is a nontrivial point, so I'll unpack it a bit here.

It is important that, to the extent possible, we use date serial numbers and not text strings to represent the periods. As an example, it is far better to use the date value 1/1/2014 than the text string January. This is because the date value enables us to perform date-driven calculations. Date values are more flexible and set us up to win long term. Plus, with simple formatting techniques we can display the date value in a variety of ways—for example, displaying just the month name, January. In contrast, if we set up a report header with a text value, such as January, we are stuck. We can't easily use it in formulas, nor can we easily update it to February next month. To summarize, the header value should be a date so that we can compute it, use it in formulas, and use formatting to display it in the preferred format.

We use formulas to populate dynamic report headers, and the functions EOMONTH and DATE, covered previously, can help. When we use a SUMIFS function to compute the report values based on the column header date value, then whenever that value changes the report values are updated accordingly. Extending this idea to multicolumn reports, we build the report so that each column header is a formula, and each report value in each column is based on the appropriate header value. Wow, we quickly realize monthly updates will be fast and easy.

OK, enough talk—let's dig into a juicy example.

## EXAMPLE

Let's get some hands-on practice.

 **PRACTICE**

To work along, please refer to *Dynamic Headers.xlsx.*

**VIDEO**

To watch the solutions video, please visit the Excel University Video Library.

## EXERCISE 1—DEPARTMENT REPORT

In this exercise, we'll create a three-month department report.

 **PRACTICE**

To work along, please refer to the Exercise 1 worksheet.

In this worksheet, we'll summarize the transaction data stored in the *tbl_data* table and allow the user to enter the report's start date. The first report column should present values for the start date's month, and the remaining two columns for the subsequent two months.

We will compute the report headers using formulas. We will then compute the report values based on the header date in each column. A partial report is shown in Figure 43 below.

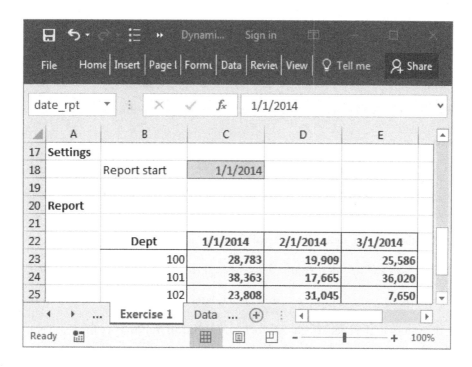

**Figure 43**

The report start input cell is named *date_rpt.* The column headers are easily computed with the EOMONTH function. To compute the first column header in *C22*, we use the following formula:

```
=EOMONTH(date_rpt,-1)+1
```

**Where:**

- **EOMONTH(date_rpt,-1)** returns the last day of the previous month.

- **Where:**

  - **date_rpt** is the report start date.

  - **-1** tells Excel to go to the prior month.

- **+1** adds one day to the results of the EOMONTH function and thus returns the first day of the month of the report start date.

Please note that the EOMONTH function above returns a date with the day value equal to 1. This is important to note so that when we write the SUMIFS function momentarily, we can write it accordingly.

We can then use the following formula to compute the second report column header cell *D22* and fill it right to the last column header cell:

```
=EOMONTH(C22,0)+1
```

**Where:**

- **EOMONTH(C22,0)** returns the last day of the first report column.

- **Where:**

  - **C22** is the date obtained from the first report header column. Note the use of a relative cell reference so that when we fill it right, we'll reference the value in the column to the left throughout the report.

  - **0** tells Excel to get the last day of the month.

- **+1** tells Excel to add one day, resulting in the first day of the next month.

Now we should be able to enter a different report start date, and the headers should update.

As you can see, the values in the header cells are formatted with an mmm-yyyy format. I simply changed the format so that the day is not displayed, which cleans it up a bit. Alternatively, you could have used the mmmm cell format to display the month names fully spelled out, or, any other desired date format.

**NOTE**

When accountants think about month-end reports, we tend to think about the last day of the month and feel compelled to use it in column headers. However, when we use formatting to hide the day, then the day we compute is irrelevant to report users, since they don't see it. I personally compute and store the first day rather than last day of the month in column headers. I've found it convenient, since months always have a day 1 but have various month end days. If you are going to display the day in the column header, then you'll probably want to compute the last day of that month and write the SUMIFS function accordingly. For this chapter, I'll compute the column headers using day 1, but if you prefer to use the last day of the month instead, that's fine; just be sure to update the SUMIFS functions.

To compute the department totals, we rely on our familiar friend SUMIFS. Logically we need to tell the SUMIFS function to add up the amount column and to include only those rows where the department is equal to our department, the date is greater than or equal to the report column header date, and the date is less than or equal to the last day of the month of the column header date.

To compute the first value, which is the first department in the first report column, or cell *C23* in Figure 43 above, we use the following formula:

```
=SUMIFS(tbl_data[Amount],

tbl_data[DeptNum],$B23,

tbl_data[Date],">="&C$22,

tbl_data[Date],"<="&EOMONTH(C$22,0))
```

**Where:**

- **tbl_data[Amount]** is the column of numbers to add, the amount column.

- **tbl_data[DeptNum]** is the first criteria range, the department number column.

- **$B23** is the first criteria, the first department number cell. Note the use of a mixed cell reference. Since the column is an absolute reference, as the formula is filled right the reference will stay fixed on the department column. Since the row reference is relative, as the formula is filled down the remaining formulas will use the department from the formula row.

- **tbl_data[Date]** is the second criteria range, the date column.

- **">="&C$22** is the second criteria, a concatenation of the greater than or equal to comparison operator and the date stored in the report column header. Note the use of a mixed cell reference. The column reference is relative, so that as the formula is filled to the right, the reference will also slide to the right, ensuring that each column uses the proper header date value. The row reference is absolute, so that as the formula is filled down, the reference will stay fixed on the header row.

- **tbl_data[Date]** is the third criteria range, the date column.

- **"<="&EOMONTH(C$22,0)** is the third criteria, a concatenation of the less than or equal to comparison operator and the last day of the month of the column header date value, as computed by the EOMONTH function.

We should be able to copy this formula to all remaining cells within the report, and we should be good. Changing the report start date updates the headers, and the SUMIFS formulas update the report values based on the new header values. Did yours work? Great job! This is too fun!

## STRUCTURED TABLE REFERENCES AND FILLING RIGHT

Before we move along, I want to discuss the mechanics for how the SUMIFS formula is filled right. Let's assume that you wrote the formula in the first column first and then filled it down, and it worked. You'll next need to fill the formulas to the right. There are several different ways to fill right, and Excel updates structured table references depending on the method you choose.

Excel's implementation of this is a bit quirky, so I just want to dig into it briefly. Let's consider the following three ways to fill a formula right:

- Use the Fill command.

- Drag the fill handle.

- Copy and paste.

To use the Fill command, you select the formula cell or range and then extend the selection to include the destination cells. Then you execute the Fill command to fill the formulas to the right, which can be done as follows:

- Home > Fill > Right

**KB**

I prefer to execute the Fill command using the following keyboard sequence: Alt+E, I, R (edit, fill, right).

When we fill formulas, Excel updates cell and range references. The standard A1-style absolute and relative references work as expected—that is, references locked with a dollar sign ($) are not updated, and relative references are updated. When structured table references are filled right using the fill command, the table columns are assumed to be absolute, and thus the column names are not changed. This is the behavior that is desired in this example, since we want the SUMIFS function to continue to reference the same columns as originally written. Just remember, when using the fill command with structured table references, the column references are absolute.

The next way to fill formulas to the right is to use the fill handle. To drag and drop with the fill handle, you highlight the cell or range that contains the formulas you need to fill. The small, black square in the lower right of the selection is the fill handle, and when the mouse hovers over the handle, the cursor changes to a black cross. You can use the mouse to click and drag the fill handle to fill the formulas to the right.

With A1-style references, the results are identical to using the fill command, in that absolute references are not updated and relative references are. However, when using the fill handle with structured table references, column references are assumed to be relative, so the column names are changed. This is not the desired behavior in our example, since the SUMIFS function will no longer reference the proper columns. Just remember, when using the fill handle with structured table references, column references are relative.

The last way to fill the formulas to the right is to use the standard copy and paste commands. To copy and paste, highlight the formulas and then execute a standard copy command. Next highlight the cells in the destination column and execute a standard paste command. A1-style references work as expected. When copying and pasting structured table references, column references are not changed. In our example, this is the desired behavior. Just remember, when using a standard copy and paste with structured table references, the column references are absolute.

**XREF**

In Volume 1, Chapter 18, selection groups are discussed and a method is demonstrated to write a formula and fill it all in a single step by holding down the Ctrl key when pressing Enter. If this approach is used with structured table references, the column references are assumed to be absolute and thus work as expected.

The various behaviors are summarized in Table 7 below.

| When Using | Structured Table References Are |
|------------|--------------------------------|
| Fill Command | Absolute (column references don't change) |
| Fill Handle | Relative (column references do change) |
| Copy and Paste | Absolute (column references don't change) |

**Table 7**

## CHAPTER CONCLUSION

As you can see, using dynamic report headers as arguments in conditional summing functions is a powerful approach. Whenever possible, I like to allow the user to enter the report date into an input cell and then derive as much information from that cell as possible, including report labels, column headers, and values. I hope this approach brings efficiency to your work.

# Chapter 22: Horizontal Reports

## SET UP

It is clear by now that the SUMIFS function is extremely useful. Thus far we have used it in a vertical orientation to operate with column arguments. For example, we've asked it to add up the amount *column* and only include those rows where the account *column* is equal to the specified account. In practice, the vertical orientation is very common.

However, I want to point out that the SUMIFS function supports a horizontal orientation as well. This type of orientation is illustrated in Figure 44 below.

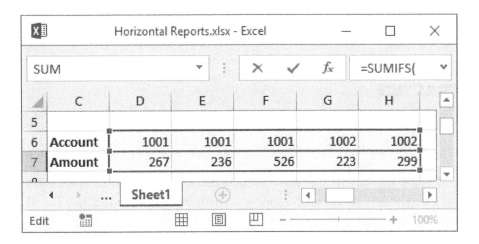

Figure 44

When using a horizontal orientation, the thinking shifts to this: add up the amount *row* and only include those columns where the account *row* is equal to the specified account. Transposing the function like this allows us to set up some pretty cool hands-free reports.

## HOW TO

You already have the skills and details needed to do horizontal reports using the SUMIFS function. The only difference is that the sum and criteria range arguments are transposed from vertical to horizontal.

## EXAMPLES

Let's get some practice.

 **PRACTICE**

To work along, please refer to *Horizontal Reports.xlsx.*

 **VIDEO**

To watch the solutions video, please visit the Excel University Video Library.

## EXERCISE 1—HORIZONTAL

In this warm-up exercise, we'll sum selected columns for the totals.

 **PRACTICE**

To work along, please refer to the Exercise 1 worksheet.

In this first little exercise, we'll provide budget and actual subtotals at the end of the report.

The worksheet contains two columns for each month: a budget column and an actual column. To the right of the data we want to compute totals: one for all budget columns and another for all actual columns. This is illustrated in Figure 45 below.

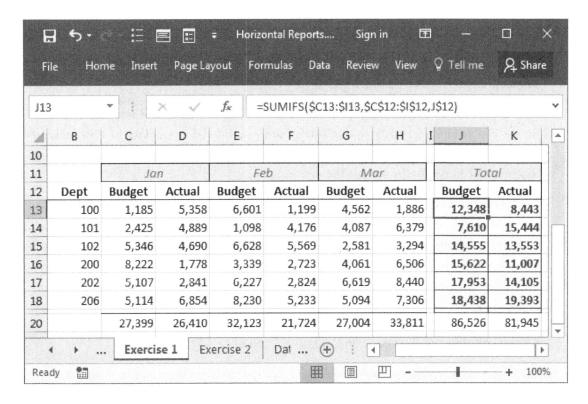

Figure 45

As with anything in Excel, you can use several approaches to compute the budget and actual totals. One approach is to use direct cell references. For example, to compute the budget total for department 100, you could use a formula like this:

```
=C13+E13+G13
```

However, this approach is not easily maintained over time. For example, if you added a new column of numbers, say for April, you would need to update the total formulas to include this new column. A more efficient approach would be to use the SUMIFS function. The following formula used to compute the budget total for department 100 can be filled down and to the right and will accurately compute all of the total cells:

```
=SUMIFS($C13:$I13,$C$12:$I$12,J$12)
```

**Where:**

- **$C13:$I13** is the row of numbers to add. Note the use of mixed cell references. The column reference is absolute, so that if you fill the formula to the right, the column references stay on our data range. The row is a relative reference so that as you fill the formula down, the function will sum the correct data row. Also note that the skinny column, column *I*, is included in the sum range so that if a new column is inserted to the left of it, the new column will automatically be included in the function.

- **$C$12:$I$12** is the criteria range, the row that contains the budget and actual labels. Note the use of absolute references, so that as the formula is filled down and to the right, this range is locked in. Also note the skinny column is included so that if a new column is inserted, the function will automatically include the new column.

- **J$12** is the criteria value, the budget or actual label. Note the use of a mixed cell reference. The column reference is relative, so that as the formula is filled to the right, the reference will properly update to the correct column. The row reference is absolute so that as the formula is filled down, the reference stays locked on the label row.

 **XREF**

> Skinny columns are discussed in Volume 1, Chapter 12.

This SUMIFS function is an effective way to compute totals, even when the sum range is oriented horizontally.

## EXERCISE 2—QUARTERS

In this exercise, we'll compute quarterly subtotals.

 **PRACTICE**

> To work along, please refer to the Exercise 2 worksheet.

This worksheet has monthly columns containing values. It is our goal to display the quarterly totals to the right of the report.

When we originally prepared the worksheet, we set up a user input cell to allow the user to enter the report starting date.

Based on the date entered, formulas dynamically produce the report's twelve column headers, one for each month. The monthly header formulas return date values, and the cells are formatted to hide the day and present the month and year only.

**XREF**

Dynamic headers are discussed in Chapter 21: Dynamic Headers.

Consistent with this idea, we also use the EOMONTH function to compute four quarterly headers. When we change the start date, all column headers are updated accordingly.

 **XREF**

The EOMONTH function is discussed in Chapter 16: Determine the Last Day of the Month with EOMONTH.

Assuming the user entered a start date of 1/1/2014, the first monthly column header is 1/1/2014, the second is 2/1/2014, and so on. The quarter column headers are built consistently and return the first day of the month that ends the quarter—for example, 3/1/2014, 6/1/2014, and so on. This setup is nice, since it works for both calendar and fiscal year reporting.

**NOTE**

Please note that the dynamic headers used in this exercise return the first day of the month, not the last day. You could certainly modify the formulas to return the last day of the month, and that would be just fine.

Since our monthly column headers are date values, rather than text values, we are able to use them in our conditional summing formulas. We quickly build the monthly column subtotals using our dear friend SUMIFS.

This brings us to why we are here: to compute the quarterly subtotals. Since the quarterly column labels are date values, this task is easily accomplished with SUMIFS used in a horizontal orientation. We want Excel to add the row but include only those columns where the monthly header value falls within the correct date range—that is, the dates that are the start and end dates of the quarter.

**NOTE**

Another way to compute the quarterly subtotals is to conditionally sum the values in the table rather than the values presented on the face of the report. However, summing the values in the report is flexible, since it will work even when the data is not stored in a table. Also, you know the report will foot, since it uses the values actually displayed on the face of the report.

Let's look at the completed report in Figure 46 first, and then work through the quarterly formulas.

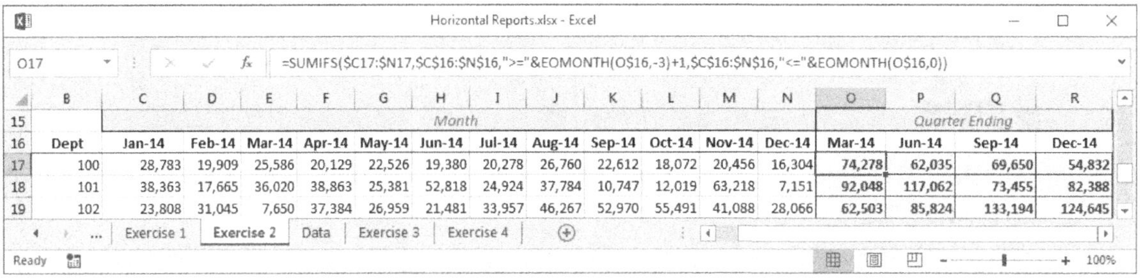


| | B | C | D | E | F | G | H | I | J | K | L | M | N | O | P | Q | R |
|---|---|---|---|---|---|---|---|---|---|---|---|---|---|---|---|---|---|
| 15 | | Month | | | | | | | | | | | | Quarter Ending | | | |
| 16 | Dept | Jan-14 | Feb-14 | Mar-14 | Apr-14 | May-14 | Jun-14 | Jul-14 | Aug-14 | Sep-14 | Oct-14 | Nov-14 | Dec-14 | Mar-14 | Jun-14 | Sep-14 | Dec-14 |
| 17 | 100 | 28,783 | 19,909 | 25,586 | 20,129 | 22,526 | 19,380 | 20,278 | 26,760 | 22,612 | 18,072 | 20,456 | 16,304 | 74,278 | 62,035 | 69,650 | 54,832 |
| 18 | 101 | 38,363 | 17,665 | 36,020 | 38,863 | 25,381 | 52,818 | 24,924 | 37,784 | 10,747 | 12,019 | 63,218 | 7,151 | 92,048 | 117,062 | 73,455 | 82,388 |
| 19 | 102 | 23,808 | 31,045 | 7,650 | 37,384 | 26,959 | 21,481 | 33,957 | 46,267 | 52,970 | 55,491 | 41,088 | 28,066 | 62,503 | 85,824 | 133,194 | 124,645 |

**Figure 46**

Let's start with the first quarter. Assuming the start date is 1/1/2014, the date value of the first quarter header is 3/1/2014. It is our objective to add up the department row and only include the 1/1/2014, 2/1/2014, and 3/1/2014 columns. Here's how this idea translates into the syntax of SUMIFS: add up the department row and only include those columns where the monthly header is between 1/1/2014 and 3/1/2014, inclusive. The following formula computes the first quarter for the first department:

```
=SUMIFS($C17:$N17,
$C$16:$N$16,">="&EOMONTH(O$16,-3)+1,
$C$16:$N$16,"<="&EOMONTH(O$16,0))
```

**Where:**

- **$C17:$N17** is the row of numbers to add, the department row. Note the use of mixed cell references: absolute column references so that as we fill the formula to the right, the range of numbers to add doesn't shift, and relative row references so that as we fill the formula down, the correct department row is added.
- **$C$16:$N$16** is the first criteria range, the monthly header labels. Note the use of absolute references, so that as the formula is filled down and to the right, the references stays locked onto the monthly column headers.
- **">="&EOMONTH(O$16,-3)+1** is the first criteria value, the concatenation of the greater than or equal to comparison operator and the first day of the quarter. The first day of the

quarter is determined by finding the last day of the month that is three months earlier than the last month of the quarter, and then adding a day.

- **Where:**

    - **O$16** is the date in the quarter column header.

    - **-3** tells Excel to go back three months.

- **$C$16:$N$16** is the second criteria range, the monthly header labels. Again, absolute references are used.

- **"<="&EOMONTH(O$16,0)** is the second criteria, the concatenation of the less than or equal to comparison operator and the last day of the quarter.

- **Where:**

    - **O$16** is the date in the quarter column header.

    - **0** tells Excel to return the last day of the month.

This formula can be filled down and to the right throughout the quarter totals range, and it will work to compute the quarterly totals.

Now that the report is formula driven, including the labels, it is fun to change the report start date and watch the entire report update.

## EXERCISE 3—BUDGET VS. ACTUAL

In this exercise, we'll prepare a report that breaks budget and actual values into their own columns.

 **PRACTICE**

To work along, please refer to the Exercise 3 worksheet.

We have a single table that contains both actual and budget values. Our accounting system generates this export with the actual and budget values stored in a single amount column, not separate columns. The *tbl_act_bud* table contains a type column that identifies the row as actual or budget, as shown in Figure 47 below.

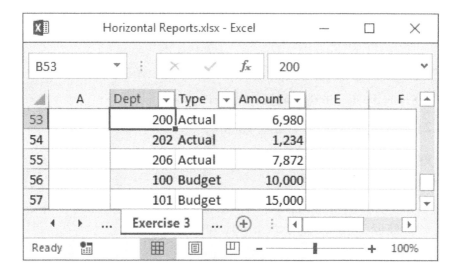

**Figure 47**

Our goal is to create a report that puts actual values into one column and budget values into another column, as illustrated in Figure 48 below.

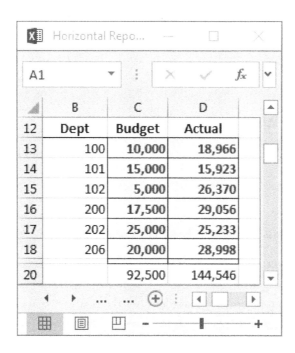

**Figure 48**

This is a pretty simple task for the SUMIFS function. The following formula used to compute *C13* in Figure 46 nails it for us:

```
=SUMIFS(tbl_act_bud[Amount],

tbl_act_bud[Dept],$B13,

tbl_act_bud[Type],C$12)
```

**Where:**

- **tbl_act_bud[Amount]** is the column of numbers to add, the amount column.

- **tbl_act_bud[Dept]** is the first criteria range, the department column.

- **$B13** is the first criteria value, our department number. Note the use of a mixed cell reference. The absolute column reference ensures that as the formula is filled to the right, the reference remains locked onto the correct column. The relative row reference ensures that as the formula is filled down, the formula refers to the correct department.

- **tbl_act_bud[Type]** is the second criteria range, the type column.

- **C$12** is the second criteria value, the budget and actual column labels. Note the use of a mixed cell reference. The relative column reference ensures that as we fill the formula to the right that the proper column label is used. The absolute row reference ensures that as we fill the formula down that the proper row is used.

This formula can be filled down and to the right and works to populate the report fully. That is pure goodness.

Notice that we used the SUMIFS function to break apart a single column of numbers from a data table into multiple report columns. This is a fairly awesome application of the SUMIFS function and enables us to create crosstab-style reports. An alternative method for creating these types of reports is by using PivotTables.

 **XREF**

PivotTables are discussed in Volume 3.

## EXERCISE 4—REGIONS

In this exercise, we'll split data into the proper region column.

**PRACTICE**

To work along, please refer to the Exercise 4 worksheet.

In this worksheet, we store the data in a table named *tbl_item*. The table has item, region, and amount columns. Our goal is to generate a report by item, with regions split into their own columns. The report layout is shown in Figure 49 below.

| | A | B | C | D | E | F | G |
|---|---|---|---|---|---|---|---|
| 11 | | Item | N | S | E | W | |
| 12 | | AB660 | 8,180 | 14,575 | 14,847 | 8,174 | |
| 13 | | AC221 | 14,391 | 16,763 | 7,912 | 8,600 | |
| 14 | | GU817 | 14,254 | 19,400 | 19,363 | 7,085 | |
| 15 | | XY101 | 17,109 | 9,327 | 17,355 | 17,063 | |

**Figure 49**

We could write the following formula in cell *C12* and fill it down and to the right, and it would properly compute the values in the report:

```
=SUMIFS(tbl_item[Amount],
tbl_item[Item],$B12,
tbl_item[Region],C$11)
```

**Where:**

- **tbl_item[Amount]** is the column of numbers to add, the amount column.

- **tbl_item[Item]** is the first criteria range, the item column.

- **$B12** is the first criteria value, the item. Note the use of mixed cell references. The absolute column reference ensures that as the formula is filled to the right, the proper item value is used.

- **tbl_item[Region]** is the second criteria range, the region column.

- **C$11** is the second criteria value, the region. Note the use of mixed cell references. The absolute row reference ensures that as the formula is filled down, the proper region value is used.

It is just that easy to build a formula-based report that aggregates table data based on both the column and row headings.

## CHAPTER CONCLUSION

Realizing that the SUMIFS function can be used for both vertical and horizontal applications is important. By now you have had plenty of opportunity to explore the power of the SUMIFS function. It is my goal that through the demonstration of the utility of this function through many illustrations and exercises you will feel extremely comfortable using it.

# Chapter 23: Mapping Tables

## SET UP

In practice, there are times when the label on one sheet is different from the label on another sheet. For example the label on the trial balance sheet may be Cash, while the label on the balance sheet may be Cash and Cash Equivalents. In these kinds of situations, it is fairly common practice to retrieve the balance sheet value from the trial balance using a direct cell reference, such as this formula:

```
=B15
```

This type of direct cell reference is a huge problem for recurring-use workbooks because of the many reasons cited throughout this text, including that the value's location may change in a subsequent period or the user may sort the data and break the reference. Thus we prefer lookup functions to direct cell references.

The lookup functions we've explored try to find the lookup value in the lookup range or, said slightly differently, try to find a label in the related label range. When the two labels are the same (for example, Cash and Cash) there is no problem, and everything works as expected. However, when the lookup label (for example, Cash) differs from the label stored in the lookup range (for example Cash and Cash Equivalents), and we use exact match logic, the function breaks.

This chapter introduces the idea of maps or mapping tables, which enable us to use lookup functions and conditional summing even when labels differ. We'll also discover that maps enable us to distribute a value in a source table to multiple reports stored in multiple sheets, even when each report uses a different label or term for the value. Indeed, the map becomes an important sheet for many recurring-use workbooks.

# HOW TO

The map is not a built-in Excel feature or function but rather is an approach or technique. The map is simply a reference table that maps one label to another. Since we lay out the map in a table, it is easy to use Excel formulas to translate between the two different labels.

Let's start with a simple example. We have an export from our accounting system that contains account names and amounts. Our reports, however, use different names. For example, the exported cash account is named Cash, while the report label is named Cash and Cash Equivalents. The map table simply expresses this relationship so that Excel's formulas can perform the translation.

Table 8 below illustrates the basic idea of a map.

| Data Label | Report Label |
|------------|--------------|
| Cash | Cash and Cash Equivalents |
| AR | Accounts Receivable |
| AP | Accounts Payable |

**Table 8**

 **NOTE**

One thing to keep in mind is that the labels need to be unique; otherwise, you may run into problems when retrieving values with formulas. For example, the SUMIFS function aggregates all rows with the same label. As you can image, if the label for other expenses is Other, and the label for other income is also Other, then both rows would be included in the formula results. The lookup functions, such as VLOOKUP, retrieve the first matching value. So, if the labels are not unique, the formula could return unexpected results. Just remember, labels need to be unique.

In terms of mechanics, you already have all the skills and functions needed to implement this idea. The table object stores the map, a lookup or conditional sum function retrieves the data values into the map, and then a lookup or conditional sum function pulls the values from the map into the report. The data flow is best described like this: the data flows from the data sheet into the map and then from the map into the report, as follows:

$$Data => Map => Report$$

# EXAMPLES

Let's get some hands-on practice.

 **PRACTICE**

To work along, please refer to *Mapping.xlsx.*

 **VIDEO**

To watch the solutions video, please visit the Excel University Video Library.

## EXERCISE 1—ONE-TO-ONE LABEL CONVERSION

In this exercise, we'll get warmed up with a simple mapping table.

 **PRACTICE**

To work along, please refer to the Exercise 1 worksheet.

The idea behind this exercise is that we obtain an export from an accounting system and then use the exported data to prepare a report. The problem is that the accounting system labels differ from the report labels. We export sales transactions, and each transaction includes a sales rep. The sales rep is expressed as a three-letter abbreviation, such as DLC. However, the report we want to prepare requires the rep's full name, such as David Cogdell.

The transactions are stored in a table named *tbl_e1_data*, a sample of which is shown in Figure 50 below.

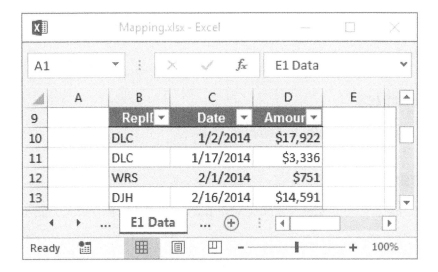

**Figure 50**

Now that the data exists in our Excel file, we need to pull the values from the export into the map's amount column. The map table, *tbl_e1_map*, has three columns: rep ID, rep name, and amount. The rep ID column stores the ID per the export and the rep name column stores the name used in the report. These two fields provide the translation needed by Excel to flow the values from the data, through the map, and to the report.

To get the values from the data table into the map, we use the following SUMIFS function:

```
=SUMIFS(tbl_e1_data[Amount],tbl_e1_data[RepID],[@RepID])
```

**Where:**

- **tbl_e1_data[Amount]** is the column of numbers to add, the amount column.

- **tbl_e1_data[RepID]** is the criteria range, the rep ID column.

- **[@RepID]** is the criteria value, the rep ID value.

The resulting map is shown in Figure 51 below.

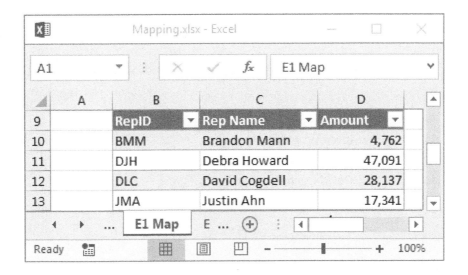

Figure 51

Now that the data has flowed from the data table into the map, we just need to write the report formulas that pull the values from the map into the report.

Assuming the first report label is stored in *B12*, the following SUMIFS function works just fine:

```
=SUMIFS(tbl_e1_map[Amount],tbl_e1_map[Rep Name],B12)
```

**Where:**

- **tbl_e1_map[Amount]** is the column of numbers to add, the amount column from the map.

- **tbl_e1_map[Rep Name]** is the criteria range, the rep name from the map.

- **B12** is the criteria value, the rep name.

The formula is filled down, and the resulting report is shown in Figure 52 below.

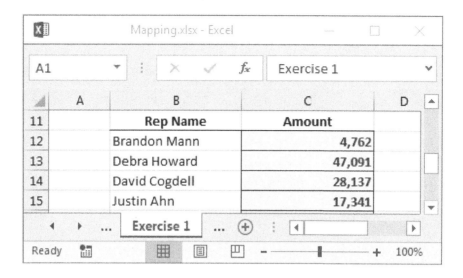

**Figure 52**

Since we prepare this report each month, we can simply paste the exported data into the data table, and the report values are instantly updated. I call this hands-free reporting, since we can just paste and go. The data transactions automatically flow into the map, and from the map they automatically flow into the report, all nice and translated. Of course any new reps will need to be mapped by adding a new row to the map and to the report.

Think you got the idea? Great, let's keep going.

## EXERCISE 2—MANY-TO-ONE

In this exercise, we'll use conditional summing to map many data items to one report item.

 **PRACTICE**

To work along, please refer to the Exercise 2 worksheet.

We need to use a map to aggregate many accounting system data rows to a single reporting row. For example, the export contains three cash account rows: Checking, Savings, and Money Market. For reporting purposes, these should all roll up to a single Cash line item.

In this workbook, the data is stored in a table named *tbl_e2_data*, a sample of which is shown in Figure 53 below.

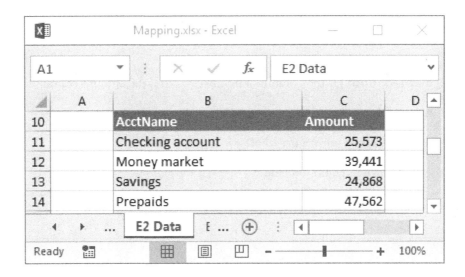

**Figure 53**

We first need to pull the values from the data table into our map (*tbl_e2_map*), which can be easily accomplished with a SUMIFS function, consistent with the previous exercise. The resulting map is shown in Figure 54 below.

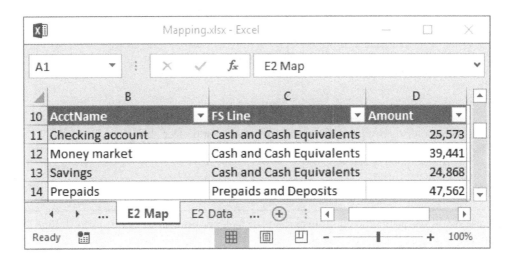

**Figure 54**

Getting the values from the map into the report is just as easy. We once again rely on our dear friend the SUMIFS function. Assuming **B12** contains the first report label, the following formula retrieves and aggregates the values:

```
=SUMIFS(tbl_e2_map[Amount],tbl_e2_map[FS Line],B12)
```

**Where:**

- **tbl_e2_map[Amount]** is the column of numbers to add, the amount column from the map.

- **tbl_e2_map[FS Line]** is the criteria range, the FS line column from the map.

- **B12** is the criteria value, our report label.

The resulting report is shown in Figure 55 below.

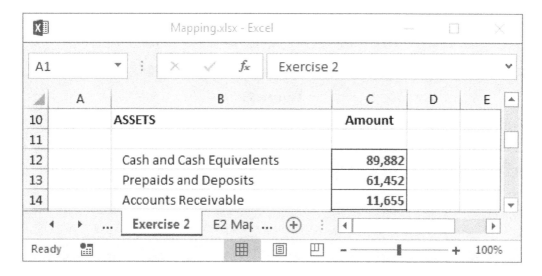

**Figure 55**

Pretty fun, yes? Next month you paste and go…and, that's hands-free, baby!

## EXERCISE 3—MULTIPLE REPORTS

In this exercise, we'll use a single data table and a map to feed multiple reports, even though they use different labels.

 **PRACTICE**

To work along, please refer to the Exercise 3 worksheet.

The overall idea here is that we download an export from our accounting system, map it, and then distribute the values into multiple reports. This time, our map will have one label column for each report.

This specific example illustrates a trial balance export. We set up the map to group each account into both balance sheet and income statement labels. We use one column for the balance sheet labels and another for the income statement labels. We pull in the data, and the resulting map is shown in Figure 56 below.

**Figure 56**

We included several additional columns, such as the account number, type, and nature. Neither Excel nor the formulas we'll write require these columns, but they can be helpful to the humans who maintain the workbook. Any accounts that don't flow into a given report are left unlabeled—for example, accounts 2010 and 3000 have no PL label in Figure 56 above.

Assuming the first label in our balance sheet is stored in *B12*, we use the following formula to populate the value:

```
=SUMIFS(tbl_e3_map[Amount],tbl_e3_map[Bsheet],B12)
```

**Where:**

- **tbl_e3_map[Amount]** is the column of numbers to add, the amount column.

- **tbl_e3_map[Bsheet]** is the criteria range, the balance sheet labels column.

- **B12** is the criteria value, the label.

To retrieve the values for the profit and loss statement, we use a similar SUMIFS formula, but instead of referring to the balance sheet label column, we use the P&L label column instead.

At this point, it is important to consider how to handle debit and credit accounts. Since this is Excel, there are a variety of different options. In this exercise the trial balance has a single amount column and reflects debits as positive numbers and credits as negative numbers. One easy way to handle this is to simply pull the values as they are into the map and then adjust the SUMIFS formulas in the report to flip the signs as needed. We use a standard formula to retrieve assets or other items with a debit nature. On the reporting rows with a credit nature, such as liabilities and equity, we simply flip the sign in the formula by preceding the SUMIFS function with a dash (-) as follows:

```
=-SUMIFS(tbl_e3_map[Amount],tbl_e3_map[Bsheet],B12)
```

**Where:**

- **-** flips the sign of the result of the SUMIFS function (implies multiplying the result by -1).

- **SUMIFS(tbl_e3_map[Amount],tbl_e3_map[Bsheet],B12)** returns the sum.

- **Where:**

  - **tbl_e3_map[Amount]** is the column of numbers to add, the amount column.

  - **tbl_e3_map[Bsheet]** is the criteria range, the balance sheet labels column.

  - **B12** is the criteria value, the label.

This is the approach illustrated in the exercise workbook.

Some accounting systems export the trial balance with two amount columns: one for debits and the other for credits. One easy way to handle this is to pull the values into the map using a formula with two SUMIFS functions. The first SUMIFS function retrieves the debits. From this amount you would subtract the credits computed by the second SUMIFS function. Something like this:

```
=SUMIFS(debits…)-SUMIFS(credits…)
```

**Where:**

- **SUMIFS(debits…)** returns the conditional sum of the debit column. Please note the arguments of the SUMIFS function are not displayed for simplicity.

- **SUMIFS(credits…)** returns the conditional sum of the credit column. Please note the arguments of the SUMIFS function are not displayed for simplicity.

This basically results in a map with a single amount column full of positive numbers for debits and negative numbers for credits. We would then use formulas similar to the ones presented above in the reports.

**NOTE**

Another more sophisticated approach to handling debit and credit values, especially if you want to adhere to the formula consistency principle strictly, is to leverage the nature column presented in the map shown in Figure 56 above and write formulas that inspect the value and automatically determine if it is necessary to flip the sign in the map.

In this example, we pulled the data from the map to two different reports. This same technique could be used to distribute the same data into many different reports simply by setting up one label column for each report.

## CHAPTER CONCLUSION

The simple idea of mapping is powerful. It allows us to automate the data flow even when the labels are different.

# Chapter 24: Data Validation and Reporting

## SET UP

When we deliver reports in a static format, such as a paper printout or via PDF, the data validation feature is primarily useful only while the report is being prepared. However, when we deliver reports digitally in an Excel format, then data validation is a huge help for report users. This chapter explores how to use data validation to provide interactive digital reports.

## HOW TO

Providing reports as digital Excel files enables us to deliver dynamic reports and to use data validation in a number of ways that enable the user to control the report values. For example, we can provide a drop-down so the user can select an option or a filter, or an input cell for the user to specify the effective date of the report.

The data validation feature was covered previously, so you already have the underlying skills needed to work through the following exercises.

 **XREF**

Data validation is discussed in Volume 1, Chapter 9.

# EXAMPLES

Let's get some hands-on practice.

**PRACTICE**

To work along, please refer to *Data Validation.xlsx.*

**VIDEO**

To watch the solutions video, please visit the Excel University Video Library.

## EXERCISE 1—FILTER

In this exercise, we'll use the data validation feature to create a report filter.

**PRACTICE**

To practice, please refer to the Exercise 1 worksheet.

The goal of this exercise is to build a dynamic report that allows the user to select the transaction type, as shown in Figure 57 below.

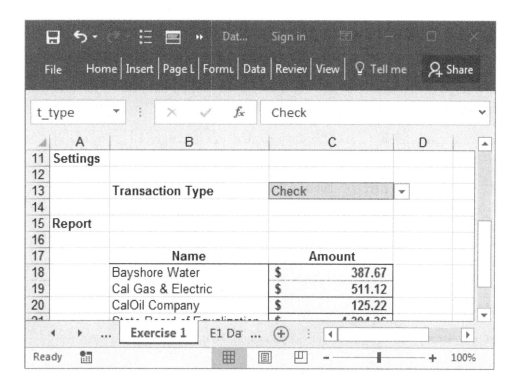

**Figure 57**

We want to allow the user to identify the transaction type in the input cell *C13,* and then, based on the user's input, we want the numbers in our report to update.

We store the data in a table named *tbl_e1_data*, store the list of transaction types in a table named *tbl_e1_list*, style the input cell, and name it *t_type*.

To enable our dynamic report, we need to set up data validation so the user can select the transaction type from a list of valid choices. This drop-down box will essentially act as a filter, pulling into the report only those transactions that are of the selected type.

The source for the data validation list—the list of choices—is the list of values in the *tbl_e1_list* table. Storing the list in a table makes it easy to add new types in the future. Since data validation does not support table names as a list source, we set up the custom name *dd_types* to refer to the structured table reference *tbl_e1_list[Type]*. We now set up data validation on the input cell and allow a list equal to the name *dd_types*.

**XREF**

Since we previously covered data validation, the above steps describe what to do but not how to do it. Detailed instructions on how to set up data validation and a drop-down are available in Volume 1, Chapter 9.

The report formula incorporates a SUMIFS function that uses the input cell as one of its criteria. Assuming *B18* is the first report name, we'll write the following formula in cell *C18*:

```
=SUMIFS(tbl_e1_data[Amount],
tbl_e1_data [Name],B18,
tbl_e1_data [Type],t_type)
```

**Where:**

- **tbl_e1_data [Amount]** is the column of numbers to add, the amount column.
- **tbl_e1_data [Name]** is the first criteria range, the name column.
- **B18** is the first criteria, the name.
- **tbl_e1_data [Type]** is the second criteria range, the type column.
- **t_type** is the second criteria, the user-selected transaction type.

Fill the formula down to complete the report.

You should now be able to select different transaction types from the input cell and observe that the report values update automatically. Sweet!

Please note the use of the wildcard (*) character in the drop-down list. Since the SUMIFS function supports wildcard characters, it is easy for the user to include all transaction types in the report.

 **XREF**

The SUMIFS function's support of wildcard characters is briefly mentioned in Chapter 20: Improve SUMIFS with CONCATENATE.

This exercise is important because it demonstrates how to use five independent Excel features and functions at the same time to create an interactive report. Specifically, this exercise used the following items:

- Tables

- Named references

- Data validation

- SUMIFS

- Input cell style

I hope you had as much fun working this exercise as I had building it, and I hope that it demonstrates an overall approach that you can use in your workbooks.

## EXERCISE 2—COLUMN SELECT

In this exercise, we'll use the data validation feature to allow the user to pick the report columns.

 **PRACTICE**

To work along, please refer to the Exercise 2 worksheet.

This example is designed to illustrate how to allow the user to select which columns will be presented in a report. We allow the user to pick two departments for comparison, as shown in Figure 58.

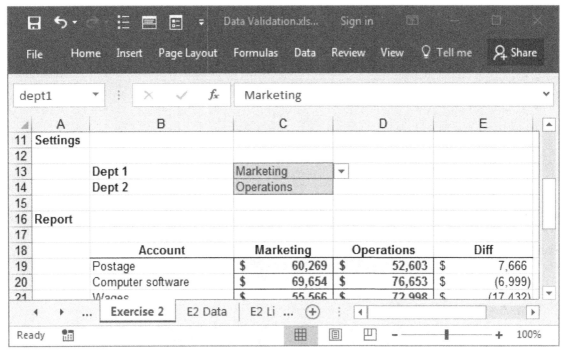

**Figure 58**

The good news is that you already have all the skills needed to prepare this report.

These are the skills needed:

- Highlight input cells

- Named references

- Data validation

- Dynamic headers

- SUMIFS

- Tables

We prepare the worksheet by highlighting the input cells, naming them **dept1** and **dept2**, storing the transaction detail in a table named **tbl_e2_data**, and storing the list of departments in a table named **tbl_e2_list**. Since data validation does not support the use of structured table references, we need to create a custom name, **dd_depts**, that refers to **tbl_e2_list[Name]**. Once the name is created, we apply data validation to the input cells to create the drop-down lists.

The dynamic header for the first report column is simple:

```
=dept1
```

And here is the dynamic header for the second report column:

```
=dept2
```

The dynamic headers automatically reflect the selected department values. These dynamic headers make it easy to write a formula that we can fill down and to the right to populate the report columns. The following formula, written in *C19* in Figure 58, works great:

```
=SUMIFS(tbl_e2_data[Amount],

tbl_e2_data[Account],$B19,

tbl_e2_data[Dept],C$18)
```

**Where:**

- **tbl_e2_data[Amount]** is the column of numbers to add, the amount column.

- **tbl_e2_data[Account]** is the first criteria range, the account column.

- **$B19** is the first criteria value, the account name. Note the use of mixed cell references. The column is absolute, so as you fill the formula to the right, the formula continues to refer correctly to the account column. The row reference is relative so that as the formula is filled down, the reference updates to refer to the correct account value.

- **tbl_e2_data[Dept]** is the second criteria range, the department column.

- **C$18** is the second criteria value, the department. Note the use of mixed cell references. The column is relative so that as the formula is filled right it properly updates to reflect the correct department. The row reference is absolute, so that as the formula is filled down, the reference stays fixed on the department header value.

Fill the formula down and to the right, and we should be good. The user can select the departments to compare from the input cells, and the report instantly responds by updating the dynamic column headers and the report values.

## EXERCISE 3—DAY 1

In this exercise, we'll continue to explore data validation by setting up a custom data validation rule.

 **PRACTICE**

To work along, please refer to the Exercise 3 worksheet.

Thus far in this volume, we've used data validation to provide an in-cell drop-down. In Volume 1, we used data validation to allow a whole number and a decimal number. It is now time to explore how to set up a custom data validation rule.

**XREF**

Data validation is discussed in Volume 1, Chapter 9.

In the data validation dialog, shown in Figure 59 below, the last option in the Allow list is Custom.

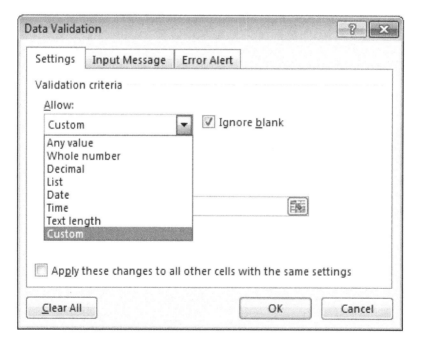

**Figure 59**

We can create some clever validation rules because it enables us to use a formula. If the formula returns TRUE, then the input is considered valid, and if the formula returns FALSE, then the input is considered invalid, and the error alert dialog is triggered. As you can imagine, this capability enables robust validation rules.

We want to allow the user to enter a report date. Our report formulas have been written to return accurate results when the user enters the first day of a month, such as 2/1/2014. Our formulas are not designed to return accurate results when the user enters a date that is not day one of the month, such as 2/15/2014.

It should be noted that there are many ways to handle this situation in a workbook. For example, we could allow the user to enter a month and year into two cells and then use the DATE function to build a date where the day is equal to one.

 **XREF**

The DATE function is discussed in Chapter 18: Build Your Own Date with DATE.

Another approach is to build the report formulas to ignore the day and use the EOMONTH function to compute the first and last days for the SUMIFS function arguments.

 **XREF**

The EOMONTH function used in conjunction with the SUMIFS function is discussed in Chapter 20: Improve SUMIFS with CONCATENATE.

A third approach is to restrict the user's input to a date where the day is equal to the first day of the month. This approach is performed with the data validation feature.

Formulas used in a custom data validation rule should return TRUE when the input is valid and FALSE when the input is invalid. Here we need to write a formula that returns TRUE when the day is equal to one. Can you think of a function that returns the day of a date? Yes, it is the DAY function. The DAY function returns the day part of the date.

 **XREF**

Pulling out the DAY, MONTH, and YEAR parts of a date is discussed in Chapter 17: Date Parts—MONTH and YEAR.

Assuming the input cell is named *r_date*, we can write the following formula in any cell to return the day:

```
=DAY(r_date)
```

**Where:**

- **r_date** is the entered report date.

If the user entered 2/1/2014, then the DAY function above would return 1. If the user entered 2/15/2014, then the function would return 15.

If we want to compare the day of the entered date to our required value, 1, we could use the following comparison formula in any cell:

`=DAY(r_date)=1`

The formula would return TRUE when the day is equal to one, and FALSE otherwise. This comparison formula can be entered into any cell, and you can confirm it produces the expected result. This formula can also be entered into the data validation custom rule formula field. To restrict entry to a date where the day is equal to 1, we set up data validation as shown in Figure 60 below.

**Figure 60**

Test it out by entering various dates and ensuring that Excel allows day-one dates and rejects others. Do you have it working? Great!

All that remains is to write the formulas that populate the report based on the user-entered report date. We want to use the SUMIFS function to include the values that fall within the month of the entered date or, more specifically, those transactions where date is greater than or equal to the entered date and less than or equal to the last day of that month. The first account row label is stored in *B19*, and the data will come from the *tbl_e2_data* table. The following formula will be perfect:

```
=SUMIFS(tbl_e2_data[Amount],
tbl_e2_data[Account],B19,
tbl_e2_data[Date],">="&r_date,
tbl_e2_data[Date],"<="&EOMONTH(r_date,0))
```

**Where:**

- **tbl_e2_data[Amount]** is the column of numbers to add, the amount column.
- **tbl_e2_data[Account]** is the first criteria range, the account column.
- **B19** is the first criteria value, the account label.
- **tbl_e2_data[Date]** is the second criteria range, the date column.
- **">="&r_date** is the second criteria value, the concatenation of the greater than or equal to comparison operator and the report date.
- **tbl_e2_data[Date]** is the third criteria range, the date column.
- **"<="&EOMONTH(r_date,0)** is the third criteria value, the concatenation of the less than or equal to comparison operator and the last day of the month as returned by the EOMONTH function.
- **Where:**
  - **r_date** is the report date.
  - **0** returns the last day of the month.

We fill the formula down and confirm it works as expected.

## CHAPTER CONCLUSION

The data validation feature is useful when delivering dynamic digital reports. It provides a simple way for the user to interact with the report, and it helps ensure that the user's input will be compatible with the report formulas. I hope this approach enables you to deliver more powerful digital reports.

# Chapter 25: Improve Error Check with Boolean Values and the AND Function

## SET UP

How do you know your workbook is accurate? This question is of utmost importance.

It is critical that we prepare workbooks that are internally consistent, with numbers that tie out and data that flows properly throughout. As workbook administrators, this is our responsibility.

This chapter is designed to expand our use of the Error Check worksheet, introduced previously in Volume 1.

 **XREF**

The Error Check worksheet is introduced in Volume 1, Chapter 15.

The Error Check worksheet, ErrorCk, continuously monitors a variety of conditions throughout the workbook. These conditions, or tests, are designed using pass-or-fail logic. If all tests pass, then we feel confident in our workbook. If a test fails, we examine the ErrorCk to identify the precise error and then go and correct it.

Let's think about different test ideas for a moment. How about this one: do debits equal credits? That condition must be true for our workbook to be accurate. If not, we have a problem. Here is another example: is the balance sheet in balance? Assets must equal Liabilities and Equity, and if they do not, there is a problem. As we build the workbook, whenever we come across a condition to test, we put it on the ErrorCk worksheet.

# HOW TO

The structure and format of the ErrorCk sheet is based on personal preference. The structure presented below is my preferred format because it can be universally applied and works well in most workbooks. Feel free to use the ideas you like and discard the ones you don't.

A couple of key ingredients make the ErrorCk work, and we have already discussed most, but not all, of them. The next ingredient is Boolean values.

Thus far we have focused on three different data types in Excel: numbers, text strings, and dates. We have used these data types in stored values and have explored functions that operate on and return these data types. For example, we have used the SUMIFS function to aggregate numeric data and return a number, the TEXT function to return a text string, and the EOMONTH function to return a date value.

It is time to explore the Boolean data type. A Boolean cell value is displayed as TRUE or FALSE in uppercase. If you enter True (mixed case) into a cell, Excel will change it to TRUE (uppercase).

 **NOTE**

> While not important for our current chapter, it is interesting to note that Excel's calculation engine treats these cell values as 1 for TRUE and 0 for FALSE when used in arithmetic expressions and in many functions.

Just as with other data types, a Boolean value can be stored in a cell, used as a function argument, and returned by functions.

I love to use Boolean values to store the results of the tests performed on the ErrorCk sheet. Each test is phrased as a yes/no question—for example, "Do debits equal credits?" The result of each test is expressed as a Boolean value, making it clear if the test passed or failed. This idea is illustrated in Figure 61 below.

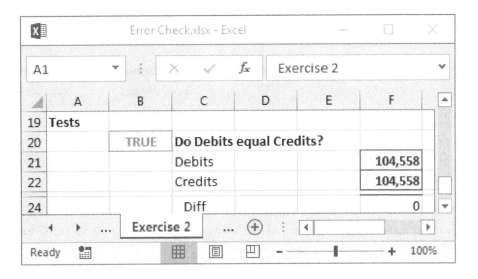

**Figure 61**

Let's examine a couple of items in the screenshot above. The test is phrased as a yes/no question, such that the affirmative answer is good. I intentionally phrase all questions so that yes, or TRUE, means the test has passed. Total debits and credits are pulled into cells **D11** and **D12**, and the difference is computed in **D14**. The test result in **B10** is handled with a formula. The formula simply returns TRUE when the difference is equal to zero. While this could have been handled with the IF function, there is an easier approach.

**XREF**

The IF function is discussed in Chapter 10: The IF Function.

If we were to use the IF function, we would probably write a formula like this:

```
=IF(D14=0,TRUE,FALSE)
```

**Where:**

- **D14=0** is the condition to test, if the difference is equal to zero.

- **TRUE** is the value to return if the first argument evaluates to TRUE.

- **FALSE** is the value to return if the first argument evaluates to FALSE.

Notice that the formula returns TRUE if the first argument, D14=0, evaluates to TRUE. When we use a comparison operator such as =, >, or <, Excel performs the comparison and returns a Boolean result.

As such, the IF function in this case is not needed. We can simply enter the comparison formula into the cell and Excel will display the result of the comparison.

Rather than use the IF function, we'll use the cleaner comparison formula for the test result cell *B10*:

```
=D14=0
```

**Where:**

- **D14=0** compares the difference to zero. If the comparison is true, then Excel returns TRUE to the cell, and if false, Excel returns FALSE.

The IF function is convenient when you want to return a result other than TRUE or FALSE. However, when all you want to do is return TRUE or FALSE based on a simple comparison, the IF function is not necessary, and you can simply enter the comparison in the cell as a formula.

Imagine our ErrorCk contains many tests, and we store the result of each test in column *B*. Since each result is a Boolean value stored in the same column, it is easy to scroll down the sheet to see if all tests have passed.

But we can do even better. We can set up a single cell at the top of the sheet that indicates if all tests have passed. This can be accomplished with the AND function, which is a logic function that returns a Boolean result.

The syntax for the AND function follows:

```
=AND(logical1, [logical2], …)
```

**Where:**

- **logical1** is the first argument.

- **[logical2]** is the optional second argument.

- **…** this function supports from 1 to 255 arguments.

If all arguments are TRUE, then the AND function returns TRUE. If any single argument is FALSE, then the AND function returns FALSE. In other words, they all have to be TRUE for the function to return TRUE.

 **NOTE**

There is another handy logical function, OR, which returns TRUE if any single argument is TRUE. Feel free to explore the Excel help system for additional details.

We could use each test result cell as an individual argument. If each test result passed, then each individual argument of the AND function would be TRUE, and the AND function would thus return TRUE. However, this would be cumbersome to maintain, because any time we added a new test we would need to remember to add a function argument to the AND function. Fortunately, there is a better way.

When we use a range reference for an argument—for example, all of column **B**—the AND function considers all Boolean values within the range during its evaluation. If all Boolean values in column **B** are TRUE, then the AND function returns TRUE. If any Boolean value in column **B** is FALSE, then it returns FALSE. Any blank cells and text cells within the range are ignored. Please note that if a cell contains a 1, then Excel interprets it as TRUE, and if a cell contains a 0, then Excel interprets this as FALSE.

In our ErrorCk sheet, we can use this idea to establish an overview section at the top to indicate if all tests have passed. This is illustrated in Figure 62 below.

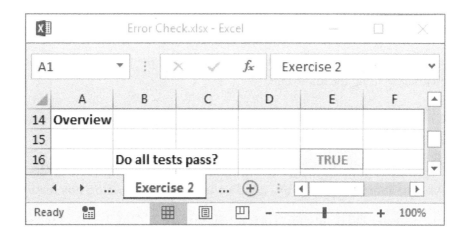

**Figure 62**

The formula used in **D5** is a simple AND function:

    =AND(B:B)

**Where:**

- **B:B** is the argument to examine, all of column **B**.

You can see that since a column-only reference is used, this formula does not need to be updated when we add more tests in additional rows. As long as all test results for individual tests are stored in column **B**, the AND function will include them.

**NOTE**

Please note that if the AND function's argument—in this case, column **B**—has no Boolean values, then the AND function returns #VALUE!. If you receive this error as you are working, don't fret; it probably just means that you are setting up the overview prior to setting up any tests. Once column **B** has a Boolean value, then the AND function will stop returning this error.

The final ingredient to our ErrorCk sheet is conditional formatting for the test result cells. When the result of a test is TRUE, we'll use a green cell border and green font. When the result is FALSE, we'll use a red cell fill and white bold font.

 **XREF**

Conditional formatting is discussed in Volume 1, Chapter 10.

Here's how to set up these conditional formatting rules. Highlight the test result cells, and then turn on conditional formatting by using the following:

- Home > Conditional Formatting > Highlight Cell Rules > Equal To

 **KB**

The keyboard shortcut to open the Conditional Formatting dialog box is Alt+O, D.

In the Equal To dialog, enter TRUE into the "Format cells that are EQUAL TO" field and select Custom Format from the format drop-down, as illustrated in Figure 63 below.

**Figure 63**

Use the format dialog box to specify a green font and a green outline cell border. Repeat the steps to use a red cell fill and a white bold font when the test result is FALSE.

Before we jump into the exercises, let's recap the key points from the above.

- The ErrorCk sheet is a consolidated place for tests that monitor conditions throughout the workbook.

- The tests are phrased as true/false questions, where TRUE means the test has passed.

- All of the individual test results are stored in the same column.

- The test result formulas don't use the IF function but a shorthand comparison that returns a Boolean value.

- We determine if all tests have passed with a summary formula on top, which uses the logical AND function with a single column argument.

- Conditional formatting is used on the test result cells, where green is used for tests that have passed and red is used for tests that have failed.

Think you got it? Let's open Excel and take it for a spin.

# EXAMPLES

Let's get some hands-on practice with our exercises.

 **PRACTICE**

To work along, please refer to **Error Check.xlsx.**

 **VIDEO**

To watch the solutions video, please visit the Excel University Video Library.

## EXERCISE 1—DETAIL TO SUMMARY

In this exercise we'll test to see that all data from the detail sheet flows into the summary sheet.

 **PRACTICE**

To work along, please refer to the Exercise 1 worksheet.

The idea behind this exercise is to illustrate how to create a test to ensure that data flows properly through a workbook. If you have one worksheet that stores the transaction detail and another sheet that summarizes the detail, you want to make sure that all transactions on the detail sheet make it to the summary sheet. If not, there may be a problem.

This is a perfect test for our ErrorCk sheet.

The detail is stored in a table named *tbl_e1_detail*, and the summary table named *tbl_e1_summary* uses the SUMIFS function to aggregate the detail. We need to ensure that all data on the detail table flows through to the summary table. The ErrorCk is illustrated in Figure 64 below.

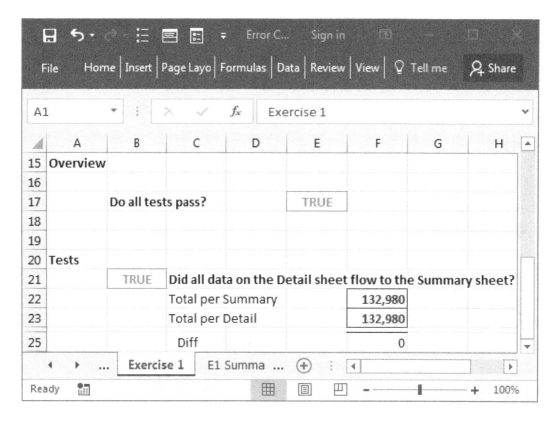

**Figure 64**

We can retrieve the total from the summary table by using the following formula in cell *F22*:

```
=SUM(tbl_e1_summary[Amount])
```

**Where:**

- **tbl_e1_summary[Amount]** is the column to add, the amount column of the summary table.

We can use a similar function to retrieve the total from the detail table.

We can compute the difference between these two amounts, as shown in *F25* in the screenshot above. In *B21*, we compute the test result with a simple comparison formula:

```
=F25=0
```

We prepare the ErrorCk overview so that we can quickly verify that all tests passed by using the following formula in cell *E17*:

```
=AND(B:B)
```

 **NOTE**

This ErrorCk sheet has only a single test, so it is probably unnecessary to have an overview. However, this idea is useful in practice when using many tests.

Last, we slap in some conditional formatting to make the worksheet look pretty. We use green for TRUE values and red for FALSE values.

And there you have it! We've created our first industrial-strength ErrorCk. This structure can easily expand to incorporate many tests.

One of the biggest ErrorCk sheets I've seen is when I was working with an Excel coaching client of mine. I asked him to work on setting up a comprehensive ErrorCk sheet, and by our next session he had written over 250 tests. That was impressive!

## EXERCISE 2—DEBITS AND CREDITS

In this exercise, we'll test to ensure that debits equal credits.

 **PRACTICE**

To work along, please refer to the Exercise 2 worksheet.

The idea behind this exercise is to set up a test that checks for internal consistency. We know that debits must equal credits on our trial balance, and if this basic test fails, we know we have a problem. Thus we'll set up a test for this on our ErrorCk sheet.

The basic structure is the same as the previous exercise. The trial balance is stored in a table named *tbl_e2_tb*. We use a SUM function to return the total of the debit column:

```
=SUM(tbl_e2_tb[Debit])
```

**Where:**

- **tbl_e2_tb[Debit]** is the range to sum, the debit column.

We use a similar function to return the sum of the credit column. We compute the difference and then set up a formula that compares the difference to zero, returning TRUE if the difference is equal to zero and returning FALSE otherwise.

We set up the overview with the AND function, apply some conditional formatting, and we're good.

## EXERCISE 3—TIE OUTS

In this exercise, we'll set up an ErrorCk to tie out our financials.

 **PRACTICE**

To work along, please refer to the Exercise 3 worksheet.

The idea behind this exercise is to illustrate how to check for internal consistency between reports on different worksheets. We have three financial statement worksheets: the balance sheet, the profit and loss, and the cash flow.

The first thing we test is whether or not our balance sheet is in balance. We will retrieve the total assets amount from the balance sheet and compare it to the total liabilities and equity amount. If the difference between these two amounts is zero, then we know our balance sheet is in balance.

We need to retrieve the total assets amount from the balance sheet. This can be done with a simple direct cell reference, such as this one:

```
='E3 BSheet'!C14
```

**Where:**

- **'E3 BSheet'!C14** is the cell reference to the total assets on the balance sheet worksheet.

Using a direct cell reference like this is probably fine, but I prefer to use lookup formulas to retrieve the value. If the worksheet structure changes, the user sorts the data, or values are pasted in, then I can rely on the lookup function to return total assets, regardless of which row the value is in. The following formula would do the trick:

```
=VLOOKUP(C18,'E3 BSheet'!B:C,2,0)
```

**Where:**

- **C18** is the lookup value, the cell reference to the label Total Assets.

- **'E3 BSheet'!B:C** is the lookup range, a column-only reference to the balance sheet.

- **2** is the column that has the value to return, the amount column.

- **0** tells Excel we want exact match logic, not a range lookup.

We can use a similar lookup function to retrieve total liabilities and equity. Then we can compute the difference and compare it to zero.

The next condition to test is if the net income per the profit and loss statement ties to the net income per the balance sheet. We retrieve the net income from the profit and loss worksheet using a lookup function. We retrieve the net income from the balance sheet as well and then compute the difference. We compare this difference to zero, and that completes the test.

The final condition to test is if the cash per the balance sheet ties to the cash per the cash flow statement. We use lookup functions to retrieve the values from the respective reports, compute the difference, and compare the difference to zero.

We complete the overview portion of the ErrorCk by using an AND function on column *B*, and spice it up with some red and green conditional formatting.

And that's how we roll.

## CHAPTER CONCLUSION

The ErrorCk is an integral component of any recurring-use workbook. It is worth the time it takes to set up, because it helps improve workbook accuracy and efficiency.

# Chapter 26: Concepts Applied

## SET UP

In our final chapter, I thought it would be fun to set up a grand finale exercise that brings together many of the items covered in this volume.

## HOW TO

The idea behind the workbook is that we export transactions from our accounting system and paste them into the data sheet. This data flows into the report sheet, and we use an error check worksheet to spot-check our work.

The good news is that you already know all of the Excel features, functions, and techniques used in this workbook:

- Tables
- Conditional summing with SUMIFS
- Dynamic headers
- Horizontal reports
- Data validation
- Lookup formulas

- Error checking

- Highlight input cells

- Skinny row

- Date functions

- Named ranges

Since we have already covered each of these in great detail, let's move right into the workbook.

# EXAMPLE

Let's get some hands-on practice.

 **PRACTICE**

To work along, please refer to *Concepts Applied.xlsx*.

 **VIDEO**

To watch the solutions video, please visit the Excel University Video Library.

# EXERCISE 1—WORKBOOK OVERVIEW

Let's check out this workbook.

 **PRACTICE**

To work along, please refer to the Exercise 1 worksheet.

Let's take a quick tour of the workbook and start with the *Data* worksheet.

## DATA WORKSHEET

You'll notice that the data is stored in a table on the **Data** worksheet so it is easy to add transactions in subsequent periods. The table name is **tbl_data**. We use structured table references in our formulas, and we know that any new transactions added into the table will be included.

## LISTS WORKSHEET

The **Lists** worksheet stores the list of departments needed for data validation used in the report. The list of choices is stored in a table named **tbl_depts**. Since data validation does not support structured table references, we set up a name **dd_depts** that refers to the table data.

You'll also notice that the wildcard character (*) appears at the top of the list. This makes it easy for the user to include all departments in the report.

## REPORT WORKSHEET

Next let's move to the **Report** worksheet. Here you'll notice some settings in the report filters area. The year input cell is highlighted and named **year**. A user can enter a year here, and the monthly column headers will dynamically update to reflect the desired year. The report headers are date values formatted to display only the three-letter month abbreviation. These dynamic headers are computed using the DATE and EOMONTH functions. Since the headers are date values instead of text labels, we can reference them in the formulas that compute the report amounts.

We also provide the user an input cell named **dept**, which provides the ability to select a department and filter the report results. The wildcard (*) character enables the user to view all departments, and the input cell uses data validation to provide a drop-down list of department choices.

A partial view of the worksheet is shown in Figure 65 below.

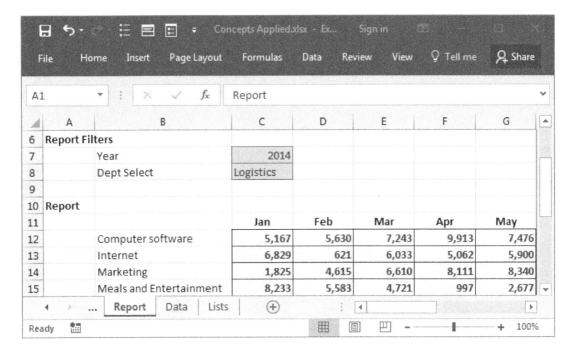

Figure 65

We need to pull the values from the data table into the report, and we'll obviously use the SUMIFS function for this task. The following formula computes the amount for the first account (Computer software) and column (Jan), represented by cell *C12* in the screenshot above:

```
=SUMIFS(tbl_data[Amount],

tbl_data[Dept],dept,

tbl_data[Account],$B12,

tbl_data[Date],">="&C$11,

tbl_data[Date],"<="&EOMONTH(C$11,0))
```

**Where:**

- **tbl_data[Amount]** is the column of numbers to add, the amount column.

- **tbl_data[Dept]** is the first criteria range, the department column.

- **dept** is the first criteria value, the user selected department.

- **tbl_data[Account]** is the second criteria range, the account column.

- **$B12** is the second criteria value, the account report label. Note the use of a mixed cell reference. The column reference is absolute so that as we fill the formula to the right, the reference stays locked on to the account column. The row reference is relative so that as the formula is filled down the reference properly updates for the correct account label.

- **tbl_data[Date]** is the third criteria range, the date column.

- **">="&C$11** is the third criteria value, the concatenation of the greater than or equal to comparison operator and the date column header. Note the use of a mixed cell reference. The column reference is relative, so that as we fill the formula to the right the reference properly updates to reflect the correct column. The row reference is absolute so that as we fill the formula down the reference stays locked on to the column header row.

- **tbl_data[Date]** is the fourth criteria range, the date column.

- **"<="&EOMONTH(C$11,0)** is the fourth criteria value, the concatenation of the less than or equal to comparison operator and the last day of the month of the date in the column header, as computed by the EOMONTH function.

- **Where:**

  - **C$11** is the date in the column header. Note the use of a mixed cell reference. The column reference is relative so that as the formula is filled to the right, it properly updates to reflect the correct column. The row reference is absolute so that as the formula is filled down, it stays fixed on the column header row.

  - **0** tells the function to return the last day of the month.

Now that the formula has been filled down and to the right, the full report is populated. We can select different departments from the drop-down list, and the report will update. We can select the wildcard (*) from the drop-down list to select all departments.

## ERRORCK WORKSHEET

If we check out the *ErrorCk* sheet, we'll notice the use of conditional formatting for the test result and overview cells. We test to ensure that the data flows properly from the data sheet to the report sheet.

We used a VLOOKUP function to retrieve the report total. One thing to note about the formula is that the lookup value is stored in a cell rather than hard-coded in the function. This is preferred because the lookup value is clear to the user (not buried in the formula) and easy to update in the future (no formula edit is needed).

The SUMIFS function was used to retrieve the data total. One thing to note about the formula is that we use the filter selections made on the report sheet. Since we allowed the user to filter the report, we needed to use the same filter choices when computing the data total in order to determine the expected total.

Since only a single test was evaluated, the overview section was probably unnecessary. However, in practice, an overview section makes it easy to incorporate additional tests in the future.

## WRAP-UP

And that, my friend, is pretty much the tour of this workbook.

There is another practice file available that allows you to prepare the workbook from scratch, including all the various elements—for example, setting up the tables, named references, input cells, data validation, dynamic headers, and so on. If you are up for it, I'm sure you would have a blast working through it.

 **PRACTICE**

If you'd like to build this workbook from scratch, please refer to the *Concepts Applied Blank.xlsx* workbook.

## CHAPTER CONCLUSION

My goal was to provide a workbook that resembles a typical hands-free reporting workbook. When updated data is pasted into the workbook, the report values are refreshed accordingly.

The exciting news is that in a subsequent volume, we'll even automate the import of data into the data sheet. If you can't wait for that, explore Excel's External Data feature.

 **XREF**

The External Data feature is discussed in Volume 3, Chapter 22.

The combination of storing transactions in a table and pulling the values into a formula-based report is potent and puts us in a position to later capitalize on the external data feature. To me, this workbook represents an ideal structure for hands-free reporting workbooks, and I hope some of the ideas are useful in your work.

# Conclusion

Have you ever wanted to have a superpower like your favorite superhero? For me, I've always wanted to fly like Superman. It may just be me, but I feel like Excel provides me with some kind of superpower. I mean, with Excel I feel like I can accomplish the work of many people. Do you feel that way too?

It has certainly been my objective to equip you with tools that enable you to work at super speed and get your work done in less time. I hope the items discussed in this volume help improve your productivity. And remember, Excel rules!

# Shortcut Reference

The following list reflects the shortcuts presented through this volume.

| Shortcut | Action | Volume | Chapter |
|---|---|---|---|
| Arrow Keys | Navigates within worksheet and cell values | 1 | 6 |
| Shift+Arrow Keys | Extends selection | 1 | 6 |
| Ctrl+Arrow Keys | Jumps to edge of region or word | 1 | 6 |
| Ctrl+A | Select all cells in region | 1 | 6 |
| F2 | Edit mode | 1 | 6 |
| F4 | Cycles through cell reference styles (absolute, relative, mixed) | 1 | 6 |
| Double-click fill handle | Fills formula down | 1 | 6 |
| Ctrl+PageUp/PageDown | Activates previous/next sheet | 1 | 6 |
| Alt+= | Insert SUM function | 1 | 6 |
| F5 | GoTo | 1 | 7 |
| Ctrl+T and Alt+N,T | Insert table | 1 | 8 |
| Alt+N,T | Insert table | 1 | 8 |
| Alt+D, L | Data validation | 1 | 9 |
| Alt+A,V,V | Data validation | 1 | 9 |

| Alt+Down Arrow | Expands drop-down | 1 | 9 |
|---|---|---|---|
| F3 | Paste name | 1 | 9 |
| Alt+I, N, D | Insert name | 1 | 9 |
| Alt+M, N | Insert name | 1 | 9 |
| Ctrl+F3 | Insert name | 1 | 9 |
| Alt+O, R, E | Format row height | 1 | 12 |
| Alt+I, R | Insert row | 1 | 12 |
| Alt+H, I, R | Insert row | 1 | 12 |
| Alt+O, C, W | Format column width | 1 | 12 |
| Alt+O, H, H | Hide sheet | 1 | 13 |
| Alt+O, H, U | Unhide sheet | 1 | 13 |
| Alt+O, H, R | Rename sheet | 1 | 15 |
| Alt+E, L | Delete active sheet | 1 | 15 |
| Alt+I, W | Insert worksheet | 1 | 15 |
| Ctrl+Enter | Enter formula and fill it down | 1 | 18 |
| Shift+Ctrl+PageUp/ PageDown | Group select adjacent sheets | 1 | 18 |
| F9 | Convert formula text to evaluated result | 2 | 2 |
| Alt+E, I, D | Fill down | 2 | 2 |
| Ctrl+D | Fill down | 2 | 2 |
| Alt+E, I, R | Fill right | 2 | 2 |
| Ctrl+R | Fill right | 2 | 2 |
| Ctrl+C | Copy | 2 | 2 |
| Ctrl+V | Paste | 2 | 2 |
| Alt+E, S | Paste special | 2 | 2 |
| Ctrl+Alt+V | Paste special | 2 | 2 |
| Ctrl+Home | Jump to A1 | 2 | 2 |
| Shift+Space | Select entire row | 2 | 2 |
| Alt+E, D | Delete selected row or column | 2 | 2 |
| Ctrl+- | Delete selected row or column | 2 | 2 |

| | | | |
|---|---|---|---|
| **Alt+I, C** | Insert column | 2 | 2 |
| **Alt+H, I, C** | Insert column | 2 | 2 |
| **Ctrl+Space** | Select entire column | 2 | 2 |
| **Ctrl+Shift+Space** | Select all cells | 2 | 2 |
| **Alt+O, R, E** | Format row height | 2 | 2 |
| **Alt+H, 6** | Increase indent | 2 | 14 |
| **Alt+H, 5** | Decrease indent | 2 | 14 |
| **Alt+O, D** | Conditional Formatting | 2 | 25 |

# Index

24264240R00161

Made in the USA
Columbia, SC
21 August 2018